Protecting Patient
Information

Protecting Patient Information

A Decision-Maker's Guide to Risk, Prevention, and Damage Control

Paul Cerrato

Jason Andress, Technical Editor

AMSTERDAM • BOSTON • HEIDELBERG • LONDON
NEW YORK • OXFORD • PARIS • SAN DIEGO
SAN FRANCISCO • SINGAPORE • SYDNEY • TOKYO
Syngress is an imprint of Elsevier

Syngress is an imprint of Elsevier
50 Hampshire Street, 5th Floor, Cambridge, MA 02139, USA

Notices
Knowledge and best practice in this field are constantly changing. As new research and experience broaden our understanding, changes in research methods, professional practices, or medical treatment may become necessary.

Practitioners and researchers must always rely on their own experience and knowledge in evaluating and using any information, methods, compounds, or experiments described herein. In using such information or methods they should be mindful of their own safety and the safety of others, including parties for whom they have a professional responsibility.

To the fullest extent of the law, neither the Publisher nor the authors, contributors, or editors, assume any liability for any injury and/or damage to persons or property as a matter of products liability, negligence or otherwise, or from any use or operation of any methods, products, instructions, or ideas contained in the material herein.

British Library Cataloguing-in-Publication Data
A catalogue record for this book is available from the British Library

Library of Congress Cataloging-in-Publication Data
A catalog record for this book is available from the Library of Congress

ISBN: 978-0-12-804392-9

For information on all Syngress publications
visit our website at https://www.elsevier.com/

  Working together
to grow libraries in
developing countries

www.elsevier.com • www.bookaid.org

Publisher: Todd Green
Acquisition Editor: Brian Romer
Editorial Project Manager: Anna Valutkevich
Project Manager: Priya Kumaraguruparan
Designer: Mark Rogers

Typeset by Thomson Digital

Disclaimer

The information in this book should not be regarded as legal advice but as educational content only. Readers should consult their legal or other professional advisors before deciding how to apply this information in the work place. Similarly, any mention of commercial entities should not be regarded as endorsements by the author but is provided for educational purposes only.

This book is dedicated to Kathy, Dan, and Jessi,
my fortress in an insecure world.

Contents

ABOUT THE AUTHOR xiii
PREFACE xv

CHAPTER 1 Dissecting a book title 1

CHAPTER 2 How well protected is your protected health
information? Perception versus reality 3
The cost of insecurity is steep 5
A closer look at data breach fines 6
Do not ignore individual states in breach investigations 10
Fines are only part of the problem 11
Factoring in the meaningful use program 13
Calculating the cost of security 14
References 16

CHAPTER 3 Regulations governing protected health information 19
Defining the crown jewels 19
HIPAA privacy versus security rules: related but
different 22
Technology is only part of the equation 24
Enforcing HIPAA regulations 25
A closer look at the HIPAA Security Rule 26
The HIPAA Breach Notification Rule 27
The role of the Federal Trade Commission 28
Do not forget State Laws 30
References 31

CHAPTER 4 Risk analysis 33
Learning the jargon 33
Compliance versus management 34
The ONC approach to risk analysis and security
management 36
Finding the right analysis tools 40

Tapping the HHS resources..43
Beware the "required" versus "addressable" confusion...............45
Moving beyond a checklist of security questions..........................47
References..49

CHAPTER 5   Reducing the risk of a data breach 51
Seeing the larger picture 52
The best mindset: guilty until proven innocent.............................52
Passwords, policies, and procedures...53
Establishing effective governance 56
Technological solutions...56
Establishing physical safeguards...67
Protecting big data 68
Testing your network security..70
Cybersecurity insurance 72
References..72

CHAPTER 6   Mobile device security..75
Thinking strategically..75
Covering the basics 76
BYOD: bring your own disaster? 79
Mobile device management software 80
The virtues of virtual private networks 83
Appreciating the difference between http and https 85
References..87

CHAPTER 7   Medical device security..89
How real is the threat?..90
Taking a closer look at the "pathology" behind medjacking 90
What is the FDA doing? 91
Dealing with existing medical device vulnerabilities....................95
How are medical device companies coping? 96
Firming up the firmware 97
Are medical device manufacturers HIPAA accountable? 98
Weighing your security options 99
References..100

CHAPTER 8   Educating medical and administrative staff 103
Culture before education..103
Seeing the bigger picture 105
Understanding the psychology of change 107
Managing the training process..109
What should the training consist of? 109
References..111

CHAPTER 9   HIPAA, HITECH, and the business associate 113
Evaluating the threat 114
Are you a business associate? 116
Formal agreements are a must 118
More exceptions to the rule 119
What should a business associate agreement look like? 121
References 122

CHAPTER 10   Preparing for and coping with a data breach 125
How bad is the situation? 125
Preparing for the worst 126
Managing security incidents and data breaches 127
Creating a comprehensive response plan 128
Decision making, accountability, and trust 131
References 132

APPENDIX 133
SUBJECT INDEX 139

About the Author

Paul Cerrato has more than 30 years of experience working in healthcare and has written extensively on clinical medicine, electronic health records, protected health information (PHI) security, practice management, and clinical decision support. He has served as Editor of *Information Week Healthcare*, Executive Editor of *Contemporary OB/GYN*, Senior Editor *RN* Journal, and contributing writer/editor for the Yale University School of Medicine, the American Academy of Pediatrics, *Information Week*, *Medscape*, *Healthcare Finance News*, *IMedicalapps.com*, and *Medpage Today*. The Healthcare Information and Management Systems Society (HIMSS) has listed Mr Cerrato as one of the most influential columnists in healthcare IT.

Mr Cerrato has won numerous editorial awards, including a Gold Award from the American Society of Healthcare Publications Editors and the Jesse H. Neal Award for Editorial Excellence, considered the Pulitzer Prize of specialized journalism.

Preface

In late 2015, the Attorney General for National Security from the Department of Justice convened all the CIOs and security officers from Boston healthcare and academic institutions to deliver sobering news—if you have an internet connected device, it will be compromised.

Boards, senior leaders, technology professionals, payers, and patients know that security concerns have risen to the top of the agenda. Millions of dollars will be spent on new technologies, rewritten policies, and security audits. However, our most potent weapon in the cold war against privacy breaches is education. Despite our best efforts, our institutions are as vulnerable as our most gullible employee.

Paul Cerrato's *Protecting Patient Information* is a highly readable, well-organized resource for every stakeholder in healthcare to better understand the risks we face and how to mitigate them. Policymakers and technologists will both benefit from a deeper understanding of the regulations we must comply with, the nature of the threats we face, and the strategies likely to be successful.

Today, misunderstanding of HIPAA is a major impediment to the secure exchange of information. I have heard all the following comments from well-trained hospital professionals:

"We cannot share data about patients with patients themselves—that's a HIPAA violation"

"We cannot send electronic copies of records to all the patient's providers of care—that's a HIPAA violation"

"We cannot use email or texting among providers and patients—that's a HIPAA violation"

"Our third party service providers must have 'HIPAA Compliant Data Centers' that are 'HIPAA Certified'"

"Our greatest threat is the external hackers targeting our data"

Each of these statements is false. HIPAA is about disclosing privacy practices, identifying threats, and mitigating risks. There is no such concept as "HIPAA certified" anything. We simply need to share information in accordance with the privacy preferences of the patient. If patients tell us (via the appropriate consent required by federal/state/local regulations) to send information to their personal email account, there is no HIPAA violation.

This book provides a practical digest of thousands of pages of regulations. The author has gleaned important tips from security savvy people in the field, from government documents, and from regulators.

Privacy and security are two sides of the same coin. Privacy focuses on policy and process, while security provides the technology enablers to support privacy best practices.

Protecting Patient Information is a wonderful primer for any concerned citizen— board member, CEO, CIO, CISO, and patient—who wants to understand how healthcare data can best be protected. Reading this book will save you endless hours of trying to navigate the regulations yourself.

—Dr John Halamka

Chief Information Officer
Beth Israel Deaconess Medical Center
Professor, Harvard Medical School
Boston, MA

CHAPTER 1

Dissecting a Book Title

If you are seeing this book for the first time, you may have noticed the words "Decision Maker's Guide" in the title. My editor and I chose those words deliberately, rather than calling the book the "CIO's Guide" or the "IT professional's Guide." The book is aimed primarily at business executives and physician leaders in healthcare organizations, whether they work in hospitals, medical practices, insurance carriers, or any number of companies that do business with medical providers and have to handle protected health information (PHI).

My primary objectives are twofold: First, to provide convincing evidence to show that the price of making your organization more secure is far less than the cost of not shoring up your defenses. And second, to describe *in plain English* the technological tools, policies, and procedures that will strengthen the digital walls built around your patient data.

And although the primary audience I am trying to reach are decision-making business leaders and physicians, my aim is also to address the issues that clinicians "in the trenches" have to deal with as they cope with the inconveniences, workflow disruption, production slowdowns, and general frustration that too often occur when an organization becomes more security conscious.

That is not to suggest that IT professionals will not find the following chapters valuable. In fact, I envision many CIOs, chief information security officers (CISOs), and IT consultants passing along copies of this book to their CEOs, CFOs, COOs, and the physicians running small, medium, and large group practices in the hope that it will persuade them to embrace a more robust security system. Similarly IT professionals who have worked in other industries but who are switching over to health care will find the book helpful as they try to navigate a whole new set of laws and regulations that apply specifically to the medical profession. We chose the words a "guide to risk, prevention, and damage control" because we want to focus on the three pillars that decision makers need to focus on. In the chapter that deals with risk, I will discuss what an adequate risk analysis entails. Unfortunately, surveys and interviews with thought leaders make it clear that many organizations are neither doing any risk assessment or performing a superficial assessment that will not protect them in the face of common breach scenarios, nor will it be deemed adequate by regulators should a data breach occur. And having a risk analysis labeled "insufficient" can prove quite expensive, as subsequent chapters will demonstrate.

The chapters on prevention will address several concrete measures that your organization can take to reduce the threat of a breach, and will also outline the laws and regulations governing healthcare security, including the Health Insurance Portability and Accountability Act (HIPAA) and the Health Information Technology for Economic and Clinical Health Act (HITECH). I will also address the preventive measures needed to secure mobile devices and smart medical devices, and discuss the importance of establishing secure and conscious contractual agreements with business associates your organization must work with.

The chapter that covers damage control addresses the reality that even the strongest fortress can still be penetrated. And although some executives may throw up their hands, contending "If we are going to get hacked anyway, why bother to strengthen our defenses?" that philosophy is wrong on so many levels. Ignoring the legal and ethical obligations to protect employees and patients' privacy for the moment, there is still the economic disadvantages to consider. Your organization will face much larger government fines if forensic investigators discover that a data breach resulted from willful neglect. And if that news reaches the public—which it probably will—that negligence will do a great deal more harm to the organization's reputation than had you done all that was reasonably possible to safeguard protected health information in the first place.

CHAPTER 2

How Well Protected is Your Protected Health Information? Perception Versus Reality

"Motives aside, data privacy, security, and breach response planning efforts are often not a fiscal priority in the C-suite, leaving patients, reputations—and the bottom line—at severe risk." That assessment was made in a 2012 article in *Forbes* Magazine [1]. Does it still hold true today?

Statistics bear out the fact that many healthcare executives believe that there are many other fiscal priorities that need to come before investment in stronger cybersecurity. For example, a recent survey conducted by the Healthcare Information Management Systems Society (HIMSS) found only 64% of hospitals and medical practices have put encryption software in place to protect patient data as it is transported from one location to another [2]. Similarly, a survey conducted by the Ponemon Institute, a research center focused on data security, found that 73% of healthcare organizations have yet to implement the necessary resources to prevent data breaches or detect them once they occurred [1]. A separate survey found that only 42% of healthcare providers were planning to put encryption in place and only 44% are planning to set up single sign on and authentication on their web-based applications and portals [3].

These statistics strongly suggest that decision makers in the healthcare community still see the need for more security as unwarranted. Some may even suspect that the call for more security is just an alarmist rant by information security specialists or vendors hoping to sell more software and hardware. That argument might stand up to scrutiny, were it not for the long list of data breaches that have been reported in the last few years—many of which were preventable.

The United States Department of Health and Human Services Office of Civil Rights (OCR) publishes a comprehensive list of healthcare data breaches in the US (Fig. 2.1). As of March 27, 2015, it contained 1184 breaches that affected 500 or more individuals. This so-called "Wall of Shame," which can be viewed at https://ocrportal.hhs.gov/ocr/breach/breach_report.jsf, includes some massive attacks, such as the one that compromised 78,800,000 individuals at the large medical insurer Anthem—reported to HHS on 3/14/13—the breach that exposed 11,000,000 members of Premera Blue Cross (3/17/2015), and the one

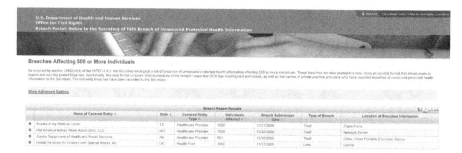

FIGURE 2.1 Healthcare data breaches affecting 500 or more individuals.

that occurred at Community Health Systems (4.5 million), which was submitted to HHS on 8/20/2014. Several smaller organizations and individual clinicians have also been embarrassed by having their breaches posted on the site. Clinicians in Ohio, Texas, and California, for example, are included on the list by personal name, along with how many patient records were exposed in each facility and the type of breach that occurred, for example, theft, hacking, unauthorized access or disclosures, and/or improper disposal of records.

OCR is required by Section 13402(e)(4) of the Health Information Technology for Economic and Clinical Health (HITECH) Act to post any breach of unsecured protected health information (PHI) affecting 500 or more individuals. Even more disturbing for small medical practices and community hospitals is the fact that federal officials are now going after providers who have experienced PHI leakages that affect *fewer* than 500 individuals. In 2013, Health and Human Services announced that the Hospice of North Idaho had to pay $50,000 for violations of the Health Insurance Portability and Accountability Act (HIPAA) because the facility allowed an unencrypted laptop with PHI for 441 patients to be stolen. In the words of Leon Rodriguez, the Director of the Office of Civil Rights at the time: "This action sends a strong message to the healthcare industry that, regardless of size, covered entities must take action and will be held accountable for safeguarding their patients' health information…. Encryption is an easy method for making lost information unusable, unreadable and undecipherable." [4].

OCR is currently making plans to not only investigate healthcare organizations that have reported data breaches but to catch delinquent providers off guard by re-launching a program that audits providers who have not reported any incidents. A pilot project that started in 2011–2012 revealed several shortfalls. Mark Fulford, a partner at LBMC, an accounting and consulting firm in Brentword, TN, explains: "The 2012 OCR audits revealed the healthcare industry at large had not yet begun to take compliance seriously. An astounding two-thirds of audited entities had not even performed a complete and accurate risk assessment, which is the first step in putting a security strategy in place." [5].

That initial series of about 100 audits found that many providers had neither taken basic steps to protect their networks, nor were they able to identify their vulnerabilities—an important requirement spelled out in the federal regulations that I will discuss in chapter 4: Risk Analysis. Some organizations did not even know *where* their PHI resided. And they could not say definitively what data had been stored in those mysterious locations.

Adding insult to injury, OCR found many employees were accessing data from unsecured mobile devices in public locations. Similarly, the audits indicated that many healthcare organizations were not training staff on how to manage PHI. The Civil Rights office has not only published the general approach it used for auditing providers, which will give you some sense of what you may face in the future, but it also warns that these protocols are in the process of being updated for use in the next round of audits. In the past, OCR has divided its approach to the auditing process into three broad categories: administrative risks, physical risks, and technical risks. In all likelihood, it will take a similar approach when it launches its next series of audits.

THE COST OF INSECURITY IS STEEP

If you are responsible for the financial welfare of your organization, no doubt one question that comes to mind is: How much will it cost me if I do not adequately safeguard our PHI? Although protecting patient information involves legal and ethical issues, let us just focus on the financial issues for the moment.

It is estimated that healthcare organizations spend about $6 billion a year as a result of data breaches. Since that does not tell you much about the cost of a breach to in individual provider, one has to look more closely at specific expenses. If your patients' PHI is compromised and a federal investigation determines that your organization shares some of the responsibility for that data loss, expect each violation to cost between $100 and $50,000. That is per patient record. So a stolen laptop containing unencrypted records of 1,000 patients can cost the practice between $100,000 and $1.5 million in penalties alone. (Although $50,000 × 1000 = $50 million, the government caps these penalties at $1.5 million.)

The Department of Health and Human Services (HHS) provides more detail on how it calculates the fines, breaking them down into four categories. If HHS determines that you unknowingly allowed the data breach and had exercised reasonable diligence, the fine is still between $100 and $50,000 per violation. However, if the breach occurred due to a "reasonable cause," that range then jumps to $1,000 to $50,000 per violation. A third category, for a breach resulting from willful neglect that was corrected in a timely manner, will result in a fine of $10,000~$50,000. And lastly, if your organization has willfully neglected to take precautions and did not correct the problem in a reasonable amount of time, the fine is at least $50,000 per violation, with a cap of $1.5 million per calendar year [6].

In addition to these broad criteria, numerous factors go into the HHS determination of how much to fine a healthcare provider, including how much harm results from the violation and the facility's history of prior compliance with the HIPAA regulation. And although the OCR is most interested in breaches of more than 500 patient records, the government will go after smaller incidents when they believe it serves the cause of justice, as mentioned above.

In 2009, for instance, Massachusetts General Hospital (MGH) agreed to pay $1,000,000 to settle a HIPAA violation that only affected 192 patients. The Office of Civil Rights had MGH sign a resolution agreement requiring it to "develop and implement a comprehensive set of policies and procedures to safeguard the privacy of its patients." The agreement resulted from an OCR investigation that started with a complaint filed by a patient whose PHI was exposed. Since the 192 patients affected by the breach were being treated by Mass General's Infectious Disease Associates outpatient practice, which included patients with HIV/AIDS, the exposure of patients' data not only threatened to expose them to the possibility of identity thief, but it also revealed their HIV status, clearly a very personal piece of information that most patients would want to keep confidential. And although the incident involved paper documents, the same judgment would likely have been made had this been an electronic breach [7].

A CLOSER LOOK AT DATA BREACH FINES

Although OCR has posted the data breaches of over 1000 healthcare providers on its web site, this is only a small percentage of the HIPAA complaints it has received over the years. A closer look at the statistics makes it clear that OCR is not "out to get you."

Since April 2003, it has received over 100,000 complaints. In more than 10,000 cases, its investigation concluded the entity in question had not violated the HIPAA rules. In more than 69,000 cases, OCR said the complaint was not "eligible" for enforcement for a variety of reasons, including the fact that some organizations are not covered by the HIPAA rules.

OCR investigated more than 23,000 cases that required changes in privacy and security practices by the provider, but most of these healthcare organizations never wound up among the 1,000+ that saw their "sins" posted on the Wall of Shame. And even fewer providers were actually fined for their violations, which begs the question: When do you get fined? A review of some of the violators who were penalized can assist executives as they review their security policies and practices.

Anchorage Community Mental Health Services (ACMHS) agreed to pay $150,000 for "potentially" violating HIPAA rule. The data breach, which affected more than 2700 individuals, occurred because, although the organization had put security rule policies in place in 2005, over time these policies were never actually implemented. Anchorage also allowed malware to compromise its records system. As the OCR report explained it: "The security incident was the direct result of ACMHS failing to identify and address basic risks, such as not regularly updating their IT resources with available patches and running outdated, unsupported software." [8]. In a bulletin released by OCR, director Jocelyn Samuels stated: "Successful HIPAA compliance requires a common sense approach to assessing and addressing the risks to electronic protected health information (ePHI) on a regular basis. This includes reviewing systems for unpatched vulnerabilities and unsupported software that can leave patient information susceptible to malware and other risks."

Parkview Health System, a nonprofit healthcare system that provides community-based healthcare services to individuals in northeast Indiana and northwest Ohio, paid $800,000 for violating HIPAA rules. (Once again the official OCR report refers to this and most other breaches as "potential" violations of the HIPAA Act.) The violation occurred because Parkview did not properly handle patient records of about 5000–8000 patients. Parkview had taken custody of the records while helping a retiring physician transition her patients to new providers. Parkview employees left 71 cardboard boxes containing this sensitive material in the physician's driveway, unattended. As OCR pointed out, providers "must appropriately and reasonably safeguard all PHI in its possession, from the time it is acquired through its disposition… All too often we receive complaints of records being discarded or transferred in a manner that puts patient information at risk… It is imperative that HIPAA covered entities and their business associates protect patient information during its transfer and disposal." Notice that the bulletin describing this data breach also mentioned a healthcare provider's business associates. (HHS defines business associate as "a person or entity that performs certain functions or activities that involve the use or disclosure of PHI on behalf of, or provides services to, a covered entity.") Several violations have involved BAs, which we will discuss in a chapter 9: HIPAA, HITECH, and the Business Associate [9].

New York-Presbyterian Hospital (NYP) and Columbia University (CU) recently had to accept the largest fine yet to be levied against a healthcare organization. The two organizations, which work together as New York-Presbyterian Hospital/Columbia University Medical Center, were fined $4.8 million for exposing electronic PHI of 6800 individuals. The data included patient status, vital signs, medications, and lab results. The breach occurred because a physician employed by Columbia University had developed applications for both institutions and then attempted to deactivate a personally owned computer server on the network containing NYP electronic PHI. Because of a lack of technical safeguards, deactivation of the server resulted in patient information being accessible on Internet search engines.

The medical center was cited for several other infractions. OCR's investigation found that neither NYP nor CU made efforts prior to the breach to ensure that the server was secure and that it contained appropriate software protections. It had not conducted an accurate and thorough risk analysis to identify all systems that had access to NYP's ePHI, which meant it was not able to develop an adequate risk management plan that addressed the potential threats and hazards to the security of ePHI from both institutions. Finally, OCR states in its bulletin that "NYP failed to implement appropriate policies and procedures for authorizing access to its databases and failed to comply with its own policies on information access management." [10].

Concentra Health Services was fined more than $1.7 million because one of its facilities, the Springfield Missouri Physical Therapy Center, had an unencrypted laptop stolen. What is interesting about this investigation was the fact that Concentra had done the required risk analysis before the incident occurred but did not follow through afterward. According to the OCR, "Concentra had previously recognized in multiple risk analyses that a lack of encryption on its laptops, desktop computers, medical equipment, tablets, and other devices containing ePHI was at critical risk. While steps were taken to begin encryption, Concentra's efforts were incomplete and inconsistent over time leaving patient PHI vulnerable throughout the organization." [11].

The data breach at Adult & Pediatric Dermatology, P.C., illustrates the impact data breach violations can have on small- to mid-sized medical practices. The group practice, with offices in Massachusetts and New Hampshire, was cited because an unencrypted thumb drive containing the ePHI of approximately 2200 individuals was stolen from the vehicle of one its staff members. The practice agreed to pay $150,000 for the violation. OCR faulted the practice because it had failed to do a risk assessment to detect vulnerabilities in its security system. In other words, it never really took the time needed to figure out just how much protection they were providing for their PHI. The group neither had written policies and procedures in place to instruct staff on how to manage PHI nor had they been training workers as required by HIPAA regulations [12].

The dermatology group agreement with HHS also necessitated that the practice implement a corrective action plan requiring it to develop a risk analysis and risk-management plan to address and mitigate any security risks and vulnerabilities, as well as to provide an implementation report to OCR. Such agreements often require a provider to hire a third party such as a security firm to monitor its progress as it puts the new plan in place—a rather expensive arrangement.

A review of other violations that resulted in fines reveals several security missteps made by various healthcare organizations [13]. Among those mistakes are the following:

- Leaving backup tapes, optical disks, and laptops with unencrypted PHI unattended, which were then stolen (Seattle-based Providence Health & Services)
- Disposing of sensitive patient information in dumpsters that could be accessed by the public (CVS retail pharmacies)
- Disclosing ePHI to a third party that did not have administrative, technical, and physical safeguards in place. The third party was using the data for marketing purposes (Management Services Organization Washington, Inc.)
- Intentionally disclosing of PHI to a national media outlet (Shasta Regional Medical Center)
- Exposing patient data as a result of security weaknesses in an online application database (Wellpoint)
- Failing to erase PHI from the hard drives of several leased photocopiers before the machines were returned to a leasing agent (Affinity Health Plan)
- Moving PHI to a publicly accessible server (Skagit County government, Washington)
- Allowing unauthorized employees to view PHI

This last breach, which occurred in the UCLA Health System, resulted in an $865,500 fine because unauthorized employees were snooping into the patient records of celebrity patients who were being cared for at the UCLA facility. That HIPAA violation raises an important concern of many security specialists, who say the risk of internal hackers is worse than the threat coming from outsiders. The OCR bulletin describing the breaches states: "Employees must clearly understand that casual review for personal interest of patients' PHI is unacceptable and against the law."

A global look at all the OCR investigations offers some lessons learned that will help you concentrate on the most likely causes of a data breach. HHS lists the following issues as those most often investigated, in order of their frequency:

1. Impermissible uses and disclosures of PHI
2. Lack of safeguards of PHI
3. Lack of patient access to their PHI
4. Lack of administrative safeguards of electronic PHI
5. Use or disclosure of more than the minimum necessary PHI

These breaches were most likely to occur in private practices, general hospitals, outpatient facilities, pharmacies, and health plans, in that order of frequency.

DO NOT IGNORE INDIVIDUAL STATES IN BREACH INVESTIGATIONS

A PHI breach at Beth Israel Deaconess Medical Center (BIDMC) in 2012 illustrates the fact that federal regulators are not the only officials eyeing your security efforts—or lack thereof. The Boston medical center had to pay $100,000 to the state of Massachusetts because it failed to protect the PHI and other personal information of nearly 4000 patients, as well as personal information of 194 state residents, including 102 BIDMC employees. This happened despite the fact that BIDMC had policies in place that required staffers to encrypt laptops and physically secure them. The incident resulted from the fact that an unauthorized person broke into a BIDMC physician's office and stole his unencrypted personal laptop. According the office of Maura Healey, the state's Attorney General "The laptop was not hospital-issued but was used by the physician with BIDMC's knowledge and authorization on a regular basis for hospital-related business." [14].

You are likely to see more states taking action when data breaches involving PHI are uncovered because the federal government is encouraging it. The HI-TECH Act gives state Attorneys General the authority to bring civil actions on behalf of its residents when they get wind of HIPAA violations. In fact, the Office of Civil Rights has even developed a training course to help AGs investigate these claims. In the words of the civil rights office, "OCR welcomes collaboration with SAG seeking to bring civil actions to enforce the HIPAA Privacy and Security Rules, and OCR will assist SAG in the exercise of this new enforcement authority. OCR will provide information upon request about pending or concluded OCR actions against covered entities or business associates related to SAG investigations. OCR will also provide guidance regarding the HIPAA statute, the HITECH Act, and the HIPAA Privacy, Security, and Enforcement Rules as well as the Breach Notification Rule." [15]. Chapter 4: Risk Analysis will go into more detail on state and federal regulations that apply to PHI.

Despite all the high profile cases in which government authorities have imposed heavy fines on healthcare organizations, a recent analysis indicates that only a small percentage of providers who report breaches and found themselves on the federal "Wall of Shame" actually are fined. A recent report on more than 1140 large breaches from ProPublica, a nonprofit investigative journalism group, revealed that only 22 resulted in fines [16]. That translates into less than a 2% likelihood of being fined.

The same report did not, however, discover such laxness on the part of the California Department of Public Health, which imposed 22 fines in 2014 alone, and an additional 8 in January and February of 2015. One possible reason the federal government has penalized so few healthcare providers is because it is understaffed and overwhelmed. The Office only has about $39 million to spend and fewer than 200 staffers. That would also explain the long interval between the time a data breach is reported and the time a fine is imposed.

Nonetheless, the Office of Inspector General at the Department of Health and Human Services issued a rather severe critique of the OCR in 2013, stating that it has not carried out its responsibility to perform security audits outlined by the HITECH Act.

FINES ARE ONLY PART OF THE PROBLEM

A manager who is comfortable with taking risks might reason that a 2% risk is acceptable and provides no incentive to strengthen one's security protocols. That logic is faulty for several reasons.

Since the Office of Inspector General's critique, the Office of Civil Rights has promised to ratchet up its auditing program, so that will likely increase the odds of a security shortfall being exposed in your organization.

More importantly, federal fines are only part of the expense an organization would incur should a PHI breach occur. You may also be responsible for having a forensic evaluation performed to determine how the breach happened. Assuming for the moment that your practice or hospital does not have the expertise and personnel to do this expert analysis, you may have to spend on average between $200 and $2000 per hour for third-party assistance [17].

Depending on the circumstances surrounding a data breach, you may also have to notify those patients and employees whose personal information has been exposed. That will likely cost up to $5 per notice, so in the 1000 patient scenario described previously that would add another $5000 to the bill.

Patients who have had their PHI exposed are also entitled to some type of protection to reduce the risk of identity theft. According to a 2012 analysis from Zurich American Insurance Company, you can expect to pay $30 per patient per year to cover the cost of credit monitoring, identity monitoring, and restoration [17]. But that figure may be outdated and is likely to be higher now. An identity protection service like Lifelock costs about $110 per year retail, which would translate to $220,000 for the same 1000 patients over 2 years [18].

You also have to consider the cost of a legal defense. If the incident reaches the mass media, it is very likely that you will face a class action lawsuit. On average that will cost an organization about $500,000 in lawyer fees and $1,000,000 for the settlement [17]. Of course, many cautious healthcare executives would naturally think twice about informing the local media about a data breach, but the law does not give you a choice in the matter. The HIPPA breach notification rule states that following a breach of unsecured PHI involving more than 500 individuals, an organization not only has to promptly inform all the patients individually, it must provide "prominent" media outlets within the State or jurisdiction of the breach. That will probably require a press release put out within a reasonable amount of time—no more than 60 days after you detect the breach.

Speaking of data breach-related lawsuits, a class action suit was filed against Kaiser Permanente because it lost a thumb drive containing medical records of nearly 49,000 patients, a violation of the California's Confidentiality Act. The relevant state law stipulates that each affected patient is entitled to statutory damages of $1000 [19].

Cottage Health System and Insync Face Health Care likewise faced a data breach class action suit alleging that they were responsible for 32,500 patient records finding their way onto the Internet. The suit, also filed in a California court, claimed that Insync, a technology vendor, did not encrypt the data or take other necessary security measures [20].

Unfortunately such expenses do not take into account the cost of a public relations firm to repair a damaged reputation, call centers to handle questions from patients who have had their personal information exposed, and the amount of revenue lost because patients no longer trust your hospital or medical practice and decide to seek treatment elsewhere. According to Mac McMillan, chief executive for CynergisTek, a security firm, "the average patient spends about $150,000 on medical care in a lifetime." Multiplying that figure by our 1000 patients may mean the loss of $150 million [21].

The HIPAA violations that occurred at BlueCross BlueShield of Tennessee (BCBST) in 2009 can give you a sense of the price tag of a data breach above and beyond the federal fines. BCBST agreed to pay the Department of Health and Human Services $1.5 million for violating HIPAA rules because it lost data on over 1 million members after a burglary. But within a few short years of the breach, the health insurer had spent $17 million for various corrective actions. They had to identify the affected members and providers and notify them of the breach. It spent $7 million to tighten IT security, which included encryption of all at rest data. (At rest data can include information that is stored on desktop computers, mobile devices, and servers. At rest data is distinguished from data in motion, which refers to data being transported from place to place.) [22]

The BCBST incident also should alert decision makers to some of the more unexpected ways in which their organization's patient data can become exposed. In this case, the PHI was located on 57 hard drives that were located in a secured closet at a former call center that the insurer no longer used. The official resolution agreement between HHS and Blue Cross Blue Shield explained that: "The hard drives in the network data closet were part of a system which recorded and stored audio and video recordings of customer service calls. The hard drives that were stolen contained data which included the PHI of health plan members, such as member names, member ID numbers, diagnosis codes, dates of birth, and social security numbers. The stored audio and video data from the recorded calls had to be manually and individually reviewed to obtain access to PHI. BCBST's internal investigation confirmed that the PHI of 1,023,209 individuals was stored on the hard drives." [23].

As I will discuss in later chapters, improperly disposing of patient records is only one of several ways to get in trouble. If you discard an old fax machine, chances are that sensitive patient data in its memory can be easily retrieved by thieves or hackers. Likewise, you may decide to give away outdated desktop computers to a nearby school or charity. Unless those hard drives are properly scrubbed, you are giving away PHI. If on the other hand, you are trashing old computers, one safe way to prevent data loss is to remove the hard drives and drill a hole into each of them so they are useless.

FACTORING IN THE MEANINGFUL USE PROGRAM

Although we have been focusing on the cost of fines, forensic analysis, credit monitoring services, and public relations nightmares, there is another potential expense that can result from lax security measures. The federal government may take back the financial incentive a hospital or medical practice received when it signed up for the Meaningful Use program and received payments to help install an electronic health records (EHR) system.

In 2009, the American Reinvestment & Recovery Act was enacted, which included measures to improve the nation's infrastructure, including the record keeping systems in US hospitals and medical practices. Under the leadership of the Centers for Medicare and Medicaid Services, it authorized grants to eligible health professionals and to hospitals to put EHRS in place that would have a meaningful impact on patient care. The incentive payments range from $44,000 per eligible clinician over 5 years for Medicare providers and $63,750 over 6 years for Medicaid providers. (Eligible hospitals can receive $2 million or more.)

To qualify for these incentives, eligible providers had to meet a long list of criteria for each stage of the program—to date we are up to Stage 3. The criteria were initially published in the Federal Register on July 28, 2010.

So far, hundreds of thousands of physicians and hospitals have received these payments, which required that they also attest to the fact that they met the aforementioned criteria. Unfortunately, many providers attested to these criteria without fully understanding what they were signing up for.

Jennifer Searfoss, JD, chief executive officer for SCG Health, recently pointed out that "The biggest problem for many providers is that they are checking off the box that says they have done a security analysis, and none of them have.... One hospital had to return $1.5 million because it hadn't done the security assessment."

The check box relates to one of the core measures that healthcare organizations must attest to when they apply for Meaningful use incentives. For medical practices, the measure requires your office to conduct or review a security risk analysis in accordance with the requirements and implement security updates as necessary and correct identified security deficiencies as part of its risk management process [24]. The Meaningful Use security regulations for hospitals are very similar to those outlined for medical practices.

Essentially the Meaningful Use program has taken the HIPAA regulations and plugged them into its set of regulations. In plain English, the MU regulations require providers to analyze the practice's ability to withstand a data breach, either internally or externally. The assessment starts with a review of your existing IT setup and then looks for threats and vulnerabilities. Once these are identified, you need to estimate how likely they are to actually cause a breach and the impact they will have on the practice. Once that step has been accomplished, the practice needs to find ways to mitigate those risks and monitor the results over time. I will go into more detail on this process in a future chapter, but for now, the point I want to drive home is simple: If the practice has not done a formal risk assessment and addressed those risks, you may be asked to return the $44,000 you received for each eligible professional in your practice if the practice is audited.

Once again, a pragmatic physician executive is going to ask: What are the chances of being audited? That question was recently answered at the 2014 HIMSS conference. It is no longer a question of if you will be audited but *when* was the answer from several health IT experts. Currently, the Centers for Medicare and Medicaid Services has been doing prepayment and postpayment audits on 5–10% of healthcare providers. But that 10% figure can be misleading. If CMS audited 10% of providers in 2014 and 10% in 2015, it is only a matter of time before they get to you [25]. One organization has been forced to return $31 million in EHR incentives because an error was found in the way the facility was using its EHR; Detroit Medical Center fired its chief medical information officer for similar issues.

CALCULATING THE COST OF SECURITY

How much will it cost to create an airtight security system that will prevent PHI from being exposed? There is no such thing. No matter how much you invest, you cannot guarantee complete protection to your records. Fortunately, government regulators do not expect it. They expect organizations to take reasonable measures to prevent a breach, and to report data exposure should it occur. I will go into much more detail on what these measures consist of in the chapters on risk analysis, preventive strategies, and HIPAA regulations.

One such measure—data encryption—is one component of "good data hygiene." Encryption, which essentially makes electronic information unreadable by converting it into gibberish until it is unlocked with an encryption key, should be installed on any laptop or other mobile device containing PHI, personally identifiable information (PII), as well as a variety of other types of sensitive data. There are numerous ways to accomplish that, depending on your resources, the skill set of the person who handles your IT operations, and your budget.

If a small practice has only a shoestring budget for information technology and there is a consultant or someone on staff with the technical know-how, it is possible to encrypt data on Windows computers by turning on Bitlocker, a build-in encryption tool—assuming you have the correct Windows operating system. Apple computers have a similar tool, called FileVault2.

As you would expect, a more sophisticated encryption system will cost more. You can pay between $250,000 and $500,000 for an enterprise encryption system [21]. The Ponemon Institute has estimated that the average cost of installing full hard disc encryption on a laptop or desktop computer in the United States will run $235 per year. But it also estimated that you are likely to save $4650 as a result of not having your data exposed with said encryption. Put another way, the Ponemon research, which surveyed over 1300 individuals in IT and IT security in the United States, Great Britain, Germany, and Japan, concluded that the benefits of full-disk encryption "exceeded cost in all four countries by a factor ranging from 4 to 20." The study looked at costs in several industries, and broke done the results industry by industry. Finance and healthcare had the highest costs, $388 and $363, respectively [26].

Unless you have an IT professional on staff or an employee with extensive knowledge of healthcare IT, you may need to bring in third-party experts to implement many of the other security features needed to be compliant with HIPAA regulations. I will discuss those regulations in more depth in another chapter, but for the sake of our discussion on the cost of security, you can estimate that it will cost between $50 and $100 an hour for someone to do basic computer and network work; if you want to bring in a security specialist, expect to spend $150–$250 per hour [27].

A 2005 cost analysis from Carnegie Mellon University concluded that a small private practice may have to spend about $10,000 to upgrade its computers to comply with HIPAA regulations; that translates into about $12,000 in 2015 inflation-adjusted dollars. A large organization can expect to spend millions for the upgrade, though estimates differ widely [28].

Similarly, one security and compliance vendor recently estimated that a small provider would have to pay between $4,000 and $12,000 to comply with HIPAA rules [29].

The same vendor estimated the cost for a medium to large organization as $50,000+. Obviously, average figures like this are no substitute for case-by-case cost analyses. The same report found that Children's Hospital of Pittsburgh spent about $88,000 to develop and implement HIPAA compliance, or about $105,700 in 2015 dollars. It also budgeted $5,000 in 1 year for staff training and promotion ($6,000 in 2015 dollars).

Since the HIPAA regulations mandate employee training, that expense can be significant and ongoing. An American Hospital Association study found that on average such training can really add up, about $22 per employee in 2015 inflation-adjusted dollars [28].

Decision makers also have to factor in the cost of firewalls, antispyware, and antimalware software, also discussed in more detail in chapter 5: Reducing the Risk of a Data Breach. McAfee, for instance, charges about $22–$25 per license for a software package that will cover 250 or fewer devices.

Another approach to PHI security is to hire a HIPAA auditing firm to analyze your weaknesses and strengths. In some respects, it is like asking the Office of Civil Rights to come in *before* a breach occurs to investigate where one is likely to happen. These companies review your existing safeguards, do their own risk assessment, and create a risk management plan. You can expect to spend up to 3 months with the auditor and spend at least $40,000 [30].

Believing a bare bones security system that includes a firewall and an antiviral program is enough to keep your PHI safe is a lot like believing that condoms protect against sexually transmitted disease. Granted, they can reduce the risk of STDs transmitted through the exchange of body fluids—think HIV/AIDS. But there are many infections that are transmitted by skin-to-skin contact, for which condoms offer very limited protection—genital herpes and genital warts come to mind. Likewise putting a weak security system in place may prevent your computers from being infected with a few common threats, but it will do little to prevent several other infections. And since "abstinence" is not an option for most healthcare providers—that would require cutting the cord to the Internet—the most cost-effective solution is a full-throttled security program.

References

[1] R. Kam, L. Ponemon, Why healthcare data breaches are a C-Suite concern, Forbes. http://www.forbes.com/sites/ciocentral/2012/12/07/why-healthcare-data-breaches-are-a-c-suite-concern/, 2012.

[2] J. Conn. Advocate data breach highlights lack of encryption, a widespread issue, Modern Healthcare. http://www.modernhealthcare.com/article/20130830/NEWS/308309953, 2013.

[3] E. McCann. Healthcare's slack security costs $1.6B, Healthcare IT News. http://www.healthcareitnews.com/news/healthcares-slack-security-costs-16b, 2014.

[4] U.S. Department of Health $ Human Services. HHS announces first HIPAA breach settlement involving less than 500 patients, Hospice of North Idaho settles HIPAA security case for $50,000. http://www.hhs.gov/ocr/privacy/hipaa/enforcement/examples/honi-agreement.html., 2013.

[5] M. Fulford. OCR audits: don't fall victim to past mistakes. http://www.informationweek.com/healthcare/security-and-privacy/ocr-audits-dont-fall-victim-to-past-mistakes/a/d-id/1317645, 2014.

[6] Privacy Rights Clearinghouse. Fact Sheet 8a: health privacy: HIPAA basics, How does HHS determine a penalty for a violation? https://www.privacyrights.org/content/health-privacy-hipaa-basics#hhs-determine-penalties.

[7] U.S. Department of Health & Human Services. Massachusetts General Hospital Settles Potential HIPAA Violations. http://www.hhs.gov/ocr/privacy/hipaa/enforcement/examples/mass-generalra.html.

[8] HHS Anchorage. BULLETIN: HIPAA settlement underscores the vulnerability of unpatched and unsupported software. http://www.hhs.gov/ocr/privacy/hipaa/enforcement/examples/acmhs/acmhsbulletin.pdf, 2014.

[9] HHS.gov. $800,000 HIPAA settlement in medical records dumping case. http://www.hhs.gov/news/press/2014pres/06/20140623a.html, 2014.

[10] HHS.gov. Data breach results in $4.8 million HIPAA settlements. http://www.hhs.gov/news/press/2014pres/05/20140507b.html, 2014.

[11] HHS.gov. Stolen laptops lead to important HIPAA settlements. http://www.hhs.gov/news/press/2014pres/04/20140422b.html, 2014.

[12] HHS.gov. Dermatology practice settles potential HIPAA violations. http://www.hhs.gov/news/press/2013pres/12/20131226a.html, 2013.

[13] Office of Civil Rights. Case examples and resolution agreements. http://www.hhs.gov/ocr/privacy/hipaa/enforcement/examples/index.html.

[14] Office of Attorney General Maura Healey. Beth Israel Deaconess Medical Center to pay $100,000 over data breach allegations: hospital to take steps to prevent future data security violations. http://www.mass.gov/ago/news-and-updates/press-releases/2014/2014-11-21-beth-israel-data-breach.html, 2014.

[15] US Department of Health and Human Services. Health information privacy: state attorneys general. http://www.hhs.gov/ocr/privacy/hipaa/enforcement/sag/index.html.

[16] C. Ornstein. Policing patient privacy: fines remain rare even as health data breaches multiply, ProPublica. http://www.propublica.org/article/fines-remain-rare-even-as-health-data-breaches-multiply, 2015.

[17] T. Stapleton. Data breach cost: risks, costs, and mitigation strategies for data breaches, Zurich American Insurance Corporation. http://www.zurichna.com/internet/zna/sitecollectiondocuments/en/products/securityandprivacy/data%20breach%20costs%20wp%20part%201%20%28risks,%20costs%20and%20mitigation%20strategies%29.pdf, 2012.

[18] D. Munro. Assessing the financial impact of 4.5 million stolen health records, Forbes. http://www.forbes.com/sites/danmunro/2014/08/24/assessing-the-financial-impact-of-4-5-million-stolen-health-records/, 2014.

[19] A. Bucher. Class action lawsuit filed over kaiser permanente data breach, Top Class Actions. http://topclassactions.com/lawsuit-settlements/lawsuit-news/11339-class-action-lawsuit-filed-kaiser-permanente-data-breach/, 2014.

[20] BigClassAction.com. Cottage health system and insync face health care records data breach class action lawsuit. http://www.bigclassaction.com/lawsuit/cottage-health-system-insync-face-care-records-data.php, 2014.

[21] M. McMillan, P. Cerrato. Healthcare data breaches cost more than you think, Information-Week Healthcare Report, 2014.

[22] E.J. Albright. BlueCross BlueShield's Data Breach leads to costly HITECH infraction, InsideARM.com. http://www.insidearm.com/daily/collection-technologies/data-security/bluecross-blueshields-data-breach-leads-to-costly-hitech-infraction/, 2012.

[23] Department of Health and Human Services. Resolution agreement. http://www.hhs.gov/ocr/privacy/hipaa/enforcement/examples/resolution_agreement_and_cap.pdf, 2012.

[24] Department of Health and Human Services Office of the National Coordinator of Health Information Technology. Guide to privacy and security of health information: Chapter 2 Privacy & security and meaningful use. http://www.healthit.gov/sites/default/files/privacy-and-security-guide.pdf.

[25] P. Cerrato. Meaningful use EHR audits: when, not if, InformationWeek Healthcare. http://www.informationweek.com/healthcare/electronic-health-records/meaningful-use-ehr-audits-when-not-if/a/d-id/1297456, 2014.

[26] Information Week NetworkComputing. Calculating the cost of full disk encryption. http://www.networkcomputing.com/careers-and-certifications/calculating-the-cost-of-full-disk-encryption/d/d-id/1233859, 2012.

[27] R. Herold, K. Beaver, The Practical Guide to HIPAA Privacy and Security Compliance, second ed., CRC Press, Boca Raton, FL, (2015).

[28] R. Arora, M. Pimentel. Cost of privacy: a HIPAA perspective. http://lorrie.cranor.org/courses/fa05/mpimenterichaa.pdf, 2005.

[29] T. Ferran. How much does HIPAA compliance cost? http://blog.securitymetrics.com/2015/04/how-much-does-hipaa-cost.html.

[30] T. Ferran. How much does a HIPAA Risk management plan cost?, Security Metrics Blog. http://blog.securitymetrics.com/2015/01/how-much-does-hipaa-risk-management-cost.html, 2015.

CHAPTER 3

Regulations Governing Protected Health Information

In the previous chapter, we looked at the evidence to show that many organizations need stronger security measures in place to reduce the likelihood of a data breach. But seeing the need for a stronger "fortress" is only step one. Before you can put new protocols in place, your organization has to understand what the federal and state authorities require. And although those requirements may not always represent the best practices in healthcare cybersecurity, they are the minimum that every hospital, medical practice, insurer, and business associate need to meet to mitigate their risk of compromising the protected health information (PHI) that they are responsible for.

Before launching into a detailed discussion of the regulations governing data breaches, it is important to realize that there is a difference between a HIPAA violation and a HIPAA data breach. Your organization can be in violation of the HIPAA rules if it does not have policies and procedures in place that instruct employees on how to handle PHI, or has not provided a notice of privacy practices to patients, or if you have not done a security risk assessment (which will be discussed in a separate chapter). A breach, which is also by definition a HIPAA violation, involves impermissible acquisition, access, use or disclosure of PHI that compromises the security or privacy of that information [1].

DEFINING THE CROWN JEWELS

The United States Department of Health and Human Services (HHS) defines PHI as individually identifiable health information that is transmitted or maintained in any form or medium by a "covered entity" or its business associate [2]. Of course, it would be helpful if HHS used plain English instead of cryptic terms like covered entity. It refers to health plans, healthcare clearinghouses, hospitals, pharmacies, physicians, nurses, and other medical providers.

HHS also defines individually identifiable health information, which it says is health information, including demographics, that "relates to a person's physical or mental health or provision of or payment for healthcare" and that identifies the individual. The government provides a list of specific elements that are considered part of PHI, including a patient's name, geographic details such as his or her street address, city, state, and zip code. It also includes several relevant dates, like the patient's date of birth, when they were admitted to or discharged from the hospital. (Keep in mind, however, that a simple list of zip codes, eg, does not constitute PHI). Other patient identifiers that HHS considers sensitive enough to protect include telephone numbers, email addresses, social security numbers, biometric identifiers such as a patient's fingerprints and voiceprints, certificate and license numbers, fax numbers, universal resource locators (URL, also referred to as a web address), medical record identifier, health plan member number, the patient's photo, individually identifiable genetic data, even IP address numbers [3,4].

There does seem to be some debate amongst security specialists about which specific elements and how many of these elements need to be in a leaked document before it is classified as a HIPAA breach. HHS does shed some light on this issue.

The HIPAA Privacy Rule cites a medical record, laboratory report, or hospital bill as examples of PHI "because each document would contain a patient's name and/or other identifying information associated with the health data content [5]." But on the other hand, a health-plan report that only says that the average age of health plan members is 45 years "would not be PHI because that information, although developed by aggregating information from individual plan member records, does not identify any individual plan members and there is no reasonable basis to believe that it could be used to identify an individual."

But another statement on the Office of Civil Rights (OCR) web site suggests that if the document only contains personally identifiable information but *no* health data, it's not PHI: "Identifying information alone, such as personal names, residential addresses, or phone numbers, would not necessarily be designated as PHI. For instance, if such information was reported as part of a publicly accessible data source, such as a phone book, then this information would not be PHI because it is not related to health data…. If such information was listed with health condition, health care provision or payment data, such as an indication that the individual was treated at a certain clinic, then this information would be PHI [5]."

Unfortunately, that statement contains several "weasel" words that can be interpreted in numerous ways. One key phrase, for example is "related to health data," another is "not necessarily." In interviews with healthcare lawyers, a former administrative judge, and several security specialists, it became clear that the OCR statement does not automatically mean a healthcare organization does *not* need to report a data breach if it only involves exposure of personal information without exposure of medical data. You will notice that the afore-mentioned example uses a hypothetical phone book in which the personal information resided, not a very realistic scenario.

M. Scott Koller, an attorney with BakerHostetler, for instance, uses the example of a list of names on hospital letterhead for the Betty Ford Center to illustrate a point. Koller points out that that would suggest these people were patients undergoing treatment, in which case exposure of their names in connection with a medical facility would be considered PHI.

Similarly, the massive data breach at Anthem, the large health insurance carri-er, has also been categorized by OCR as a HIPAA breach despite the fact the An-them reported: "The information accessed may have included names, dates of birth, Social Security numbers, health care ID numbers, home addresses, email addresses, and employment information, including income data. We have no reason to believe credit card or banking information was compromised, nor is there evidence at this time that medical information such as claims, test results, or diagnostic codes, was targeted or obtained [6]."

That interpretation is consistent with the view of Rachel Seeger, a senior HHS advisor, who believes "The personally identifiable information that HIPAA-covered health plans maintain on enrollees and members — including names and Social Security Numbers — is protected under HIPAA, even if no specific diagnostic or treatment information is disclosed [7]."

Although HHS wants to keep PHI private, it also realizes that there is tremen-dous value in analyzing patient data. Such analysis can help detect emerging infections, offer hints of possible causes of diseases, suggest new treatment options—the list goes on and on. In order to facilitate research in these areas, HIPAA provides a way to strip sensitive information from patient records so that it does not violate patients' right to privacy while at the same time offer-ing a rich treasure trove on research data. HIPAA stipulates that as long as you follow the de-identifying guidelines outlined on the OCR web site, you are not violating the Privacy Rule.

Finally, the aforementioned HIPAA rule mentions business associates (BAs). As you would expect, HHS also defines this term: "A person or entity who, on behalf of a covered entity, performs or assists in performance of a function or activity involving the use or disclosure of individually identifiable health infor-mation, such as data analysis, claims processing or administration, utilization review, and quality assurance reviews… Business associates are also persons or entities performing legal, actuarial, accounting, consulting, data aggregation, management, administrative, accreditation, or financial services to or for a cov-ered entity where performing those services involves disclosure of individually identifiable health information by the covered entity or another business as-sociate of the covered entity to that person or entity [8]."

The key point to remember here is that a business associate for our purposes is a person or organization that handles health information, including patient demographics, that can be traced back to an individual, which means it excludes de-identified patient data. Your janitorial service is probably not a BA, assuming it has no access to PHI; but your bookkeeper may be a BA.

HIPAA PRIVACY VERSUS SECURITY RULES: RELATED BUT DIFFERENT

Among other things, the Health Insurance Portability and Accountability Act (HIPAA) spells out the rules that allow patients to hold on to their health insurance when they move from one employer to another, which was a major concern in 1996 when the bill was passed. But for our purposes the more relevant portion of the law is the second part, which contains 5 sections:

- Standards for Electronic Transactions
- Unique Identifier Standards
- The Security Rule
- The Privacy Rule
- The Enforcement Rule

We will concentrate on the last three sections.

One of the best ways to distinguish between the HIPAA Privacy and Security rules is by way of an illustration. If you refuse to give a patient access to their medical data, you are violating the Privacy Rule because you are violating their right to control the use of their personal information. If you allow a hacker to steal that patient's medical information located in an electronic health record, you are not only violating the privacy rule, which guarantees confidentiality of PHI in all formats, whether paper, oral, or electronic but also violating the Security Rule, which requires you to have in place administrative, physical, and technical safeguards that prevent such unauthorized access to their data in electronic form. Put another way, the Privacy Rule determines who can have access to a person's PHI while the Security Rule spells out the general approach your organization must take to make sure the only person who has access to electronic protected health information (ePHI) is the person who has the right to see it.

Not providing patients with access to their health information can have serious consequences. If you do not have a system in place to provide that access, your organization can be fined.

So what do these rules require healthcare organizations to actually *do* on a daily basis? They are required to provide patients with a copy of their medical records; they can, however, ask them to make that request in writing if they so choose. The provider has up to 30 days to respond to a patient's request for their records but OCR also states that "As a practical matter, individuals might expect, when making a request of a technologically sophisticated covered entity, that their requests could be responded to instantaneously or well before the current required time-frame [9]."

As a general rule, your organization has to provide patients access to what HHS refers to as "designated record sets," which includes medical and billing records, a health plan's enrollment, payment, claims adjudication, and case management records. It also includes any information used by your organization to make decisions about the patient. You can deny access to certain types of patient information, including psychotherapy notes, information for use in legal proceedings, certain information held by clinical labs, and some requests made by prisoners.

Most healthcare professionals are familiar with the privacy notification that must be given to patients. That notice has to inform patients about the ways in which the healthcare organization may use and disclose PHI. It must also state the organization's duties to protect privacy, provide a notice of privacy practices, and abide by the terms of the current notice. The notice must describe individuals' rights, including the right to complain to HHS if they believe their privacy has been violated. That right to file a complaint has been the start of many regulatory nightmares for providers because it sometimes results in investigations by the Office of Civil Rights and other government authorities to determine the cause of the privacy violation.

The Private Rule requires your organization to seek the permission of patients to share their medical information with others, with some exceptions. Clinicians do not have to ask permission when they share medical data with other clinicians for the purpose of treating the patient—but they need to be especially careful that this information arrives at the correct destination, whether it is in written, oral, or electronic format. Although the focus recently has been on the danger of compromising patients' electronic data through external hacking or snooping by internal users, it is easy to forget about less newsworthy risks.

Faxing is a prime example. Although the technology is losing favor among some in the business world, it is still quite common in healthcare settings, especially when two providers want to share lab results and do not share a common electronic health record system or belong to the same health information exchange.

HHS explains that the HIPAA Privacy Rule most definitely applies to fax, email, and phone calls. The HHS Office of Civil Rights states: "The Privacy Rule requires that covered health care providers apply reasonable safeguards when making these communications to protect the information from inappropriate use or disclosure. These safeguards may vary depending on the mode of communication used. For example, when faxing PHI to a telephone number that is not regularly used, a reasonable safeguard may involve a provider first confirming the fax number with the intended recipient. Similarly, a covered entity may pre-program frequently used numbers directly into the fax machine to avoid misdirecting the information. When discussing patient health information orally with another provider in proximity of others, a doctor may be able to reasonably safeguard the information by lowering his or her voice [10]." I am often told stories by clinicians who overheard medical colleagues discuss a patient's health problems in the elevator using their names or other identifiable details.

There have been several reports of faxes winding up in the wrong hands, with sometimes disastrous results. A case in point: Quality Health Claims Consultants LLC experienced a data breach that made it onto the publically available OCR list of breach breaches affecting at least 500 individuals—the so-called Wall of Shame. Quality Health Claims Consultants, which was a business associate of an unnamed healthcare organization, mailed letters to its clients to request documents that contained PHI, including names, addresses, dates of birth, and social security numbers. OCR explained that the breach was the result of the BA giving its healthcare clients an incorrect fax number, which led to more than 1500 individuals having their personal information exposed [11].

Although the Quality Health Claims Consultants case affected over 1500, a recent incident involving a solo urology practice indicates a provider can get in trouble with federal regulators when even one patient's PHI is compromised. The office manager in this case had planned to send information about an HIV-infected patient to another medical provider via fax but accidentally faxed it to his *employer* instead. The patient, according to a report in *Renal and Urology News,* reported the incident to OCR, which eventually arrived at the urologist's office to investigate the matter. The office manager was issued a warning letter, the office staff was referred for HIPAA privacy training, and the office was told to revise its fax cover sheet to make it clear that the contents of the message was confidential communication for the intended recipient only [12].

The American Medical Association has an FAQ section on its web site to help physicians deal with a variety of HIPAA-related questions about faxing sensitive information [13]. Chapter 5: Reducing the Risk of a Data Breach on preventive strategies, will go into detail on how to reduce the risk of fax-related HIPAA violations.

TECHNOLOGY IS ONLY PART OF THE EQUATION

The HIPAA regulations spend a lot of ink outlining how electronic data should be protected, but they also discuss physical safeguards. When referring to "reasonable and appropriate" precautions, they suggest that shredding paper documents containing PHI before discarding them is one such measure. Securing medical records with lock and key and limiting access to those keys is likewise necessary. Of course, keeping locked doors closed is another obvious safeguard but not always one that decision makers or their staffs abide by. More than one medical provider has been guilty of keeping the door to a server closet open because it was getting too hot in the closet.

HIPAA regulations also put a premium on written policy statements and staff training, as mentioned earlier. All the technology in the world cannot replace a clear cut set of institutional guidelines and a culture that values patient safety and privacy. However, HHS realizes that the needs and capabilities of healthcare organizations vary widely and attempts to take these differences into consideration as it spells out the administrative requirements needed to mitigate the risk of an information leak.

HHS expects you to appoint a privacy official to develop and implement the organization's privacy policies and procedures, as well as a person in the office to contact in case there are complaints or requests for information.

Equally important is a workforce training program that educates all workflow members on your policies and procedures. And the HIPAA regulation makes it clear that the workforce does not just include employees but also volunteers, trainees, and anyone else whose conduct is under the direct control of your organization, whether or not they are paid for their services. The federal regulations also insist that you have a mechanism in place that applies sanctions against workers who violate policies and procedures in the Privacy Rule. In other words, workers need to be held accountable for their actions and realize that there can be serious consequences for ignoring the privacy safeguards put in place. More details on what the policy and procedures manual should contain and what the training should consist of will be covered in subsequent chapters.

ENFORCING HIPAA REGULATIONS

As of October 2015, there have been over 1000 healthcare organizations and clinicians who have been cited on the OCR web site for HIPAA data breaches that affected 500 individuals or more. But only 22 of these violations have resulted in financial penalties. A more in-depth discussion of the various HHS actions against offenders was provided in chapter 2: How Well Protected is Your PHI? Perception Versus Reality, but to sum up the HIPAA enforcement policy, the Office of Civil Rights has the authority to impose civil monetary penalties and pursue criminal prosecution.

As mentioned in chapter 2: How Well Protected is Your PHI? Perception Versus Reality, for violations that occurred before February 18, 2009, organizations can be fined up to $100 per violation with a calendar year cap of $25,000. If a violation occurred on or after that date, they can be fined $100 to $50,000 or more per violation with a calendar year cap of $1.5 million. The amount of the penalty is determined by whether or not the provider knew or should have known about the problem before it erupted, and whether willful neglect was involved.

OCR will also give the healthcare organization a chance to explain its action before imposing a penalty, allowing it to provide written evidence of circumstances that it believes would reduce or eliminate the penalty.

Lastly, OCR has the legal right to move from civil to criminal action. The OCR explains: "A person who knowingly obtains or discloses individually identifiable health information in violation of the Privacy Rule may face a criminal penalty of up to $50,000 and up to one-year imprisonment. The criminal penalties increase to $100,000 and up to five years imprisonment if the wrongful conduct involves false pretenses, and to $250,000 and up to 10 years imprisonment if the wrongful conduct involves the intent to sell, transfer, or use identifiable health information for commercial advantage, personal gain or malicious harm. The Department of Justice is responsible for criminal prosecutions under the Privacy Rule [14]."

A CLOSER LOOK AT THE HIPAA SECURITY RULE

As mentioned previously, the Security Rule applies specifically to electronic forms of PHI. HHS updated the privacy and security rules spelled out in HIPAA, which was originally enacted in 1996, by putting into place an expanded set of regulations referred to at the 2013 Omnibus Rule. The updated rule expanded many of the security requirements as they apply to the business associates of healthcare organizations, including contractors and subcontractors that handle ePHI. It also expanded patients' rights, allowing them to ask for copies of the electronic medical record in electronic form. And if they pay for their medical care by cash, they can instruct their provider not to share details of their treatment with their health plan. The rule also set new limits on how others can use PHI for marketing and fundraising purposes—and prohibits the sale of an individual's health information without their permission.

We will cover some of the more important aspects of the Security Rule but it is by no means a comprehensive description of all the pertinent regulations. In fact, you will need to have someone on staff who is fully informed on all the details of the Security Rule because HSS requires every healthcare organization to appoint a security officer. To quote the official language from OCR: "A covered entity must designate a security official who is responsible for developing and implementing its security policies and procedures."

Two of the most important requirements spelled out in the HPAA Security Rule center around identifying and protecting against reasonably anticipated threats and protecting ePHI from reasonably anticipated, impermissible uses or disclosures. To accomplish those twin goals requires a detailed risk analysis and a well-thought out management plan—two things that many smaller providers tend to overlook. If you have read chapter 2: *How Well-Protected is Your Protected Health Information? Perception versus Reality*, you already know that many provider organizations have not done their due diligence in this area and have been penalized as a result by federal authorities.

The Security Rule outlines four steps in the risk analysis process: (1) evaluate the likelihood and the impact of the potential risk to your ePHI, (2) put the necessary security measures in place to address the risks your analysis has detected, (3) document the measures you have implemented and where required the rationale for these measures, and (4) maintain continuous security protections, periodically evaluating their effectiveness.

Like the Privacy Rule, the Security Rule spells out three categories of safeguards needed to protect PHI: physical, administrative, and technical. The physical and administrative protocols are similar to those required in the Privacy Rule, including workforce training and physically securing devices in place. But the technical safeguards are worth a closer look.

They fall into four broad categories: access controls, audit controls, integrity controls, and transmission security. Access control refers to the technical policies and procedures that allow only authorized persons to access ePHI. Audit controls are a set of hardware, software, and/or procedural mechanisms to record and examine access and other activity in information systems that contain or use ePHI. Integrity controls refer to policies and procedures to ensure that ePHI is not improperly altered or destroyed. It also requires electronic measures be put in place to confirm that ePHI has not been improperly altered or destroyed. And lastly, transmission security means implementing technical security measures that guard against unauthorized access to ePHI that is being transmitted over an electronic network [15]. Chapter 5: Reducing the Risk of a Data Breach will go into more details on these safeguards.

THE HIPAA BREACH NOTIFICATION RULE

If you keep up with the news, you no doubt know that the number of data breaches in the United States continues to grow. Should those disturbing statistics someday include your organization, you will need to understand the HHS rules on how to notify the appropriate authorities, and how to manage the breach itself. We will discuss the notification process here and breach management in a separate chapter.

HIPAA provides a general definition of a breach as "an impermissible use or disclosure under the Privacy Rule that compromises the security or privacy of the PHI. An impermissible use or disclosure of PHI is presumed to be a breach unless the covered entity or business associate, as applicable, demonstrates that there is a low probability that the PHI has been compromised based on a risk assessment..." [16] Your organization only has to notify the authorities if the breach involves unsecured PHI, which HHS defines as information that has not been rendered unusable, unreadable, or indecipherable to unauthorized persons by means of approved technology or methodology.

If you determine that a breach has indeed occurred based on the HIPAA criteria, the rule requires notification of persons whose data has been compromised, as well as notification of HHS and in some cases, the local press. If a business associate of a healthcare organization experiences a breach, it must also notify the covered entity that it works for, in other words, your hospital, medical practice, health plan or individual clinician.

To notify patients, employees, or anyone else affected by the breach, you need to send out a first class letter or an email, assuming that the person has agreed to receive such notifications electronically. And said notifications have to be done in a timely manner—no later than 60 days after you discover the breach. The notification should provide a brief description of what happened, an explanation of the types of information that has been compromised, the steps individuals should take to protect themselves for possible harm, and an explanation of what your organization is doing to investigate the breach, reduce the damage, and prevent additional breaches. You also need to give people your contact information, or the contact information of your BA, to learn more.

If the breach affects more than 500 residents of a State or jurisdiction, you are also obligated to notify "prominent media outlets serving the State or jurisdiction."

The process of informing HHS involves filling out a form on its web site—within 60 days if the breach affected 500 or more individuals. If, on the other hand, it affects fewer than 500 persons, you are allowed to inform HHS on an annual basis, which translates as no later than 60 days after the end of the calendar year in which the breaches were discovered.

Once you have followed all these rules and regulations, do not forget the need for documentation. In fact, the HIPAA breach notification rule spells this out in specific terms. Your need to retain proof that your organization has notified all the necessary parties of a breach, or documentation that notification was not necessary because your risk assessment demonstrates that there's a low probability that PHI has been compromised.

THE ROLE OF THE FEDERAL TRADE COMMISSION

You may be surprised to find out that the Federal Trade Commission (FTC) shares jurisdiction with OCR in the area of healthcare privacy and security. In recent years, they have become a growing presence in this arena, enforcing the FTC Act as it applies to the medical industry.

For instance, The FTC's Health Breach Notification Rule requires companies that have a security breach to notify everyone whose information has been breached, notify FTC, and "in many cases, notify the media [17]." The Commission states that if your business or organization has a website that allows the public to keep medical information online or an application that is used for personal health records—for instance, a device that lets patients upload blood pressure readings—then these electronic tools are subject to FTC scrutiny. The American Recovery and Reinvestment Act of 2009 provided provisions to strengthen security and privacy in web-based businesses, which include the aforementioned apps and personal medical records systems.

However, FTC explains that its breach notification rule does not apply to health information that has been secured through technologies specified by HHS, nor does it apply to businesses or organizations covered by HIPAA. According to FTC: "In case of a security breach, entities covered by HIPAA must comply with 'HHS' breach notification rule."

So who exactly is covered by the FTC rule? If you are a business associate that only handles PHI for a HIPAA covered entity, like a hospital, medical practice, or insurance plan, the FTC breach notification rule does not apply to your business. But the operative word in that sentence is *only*. If in addition to serving as a business associate to a HIPAA covered organization you also offer some sort of personal health record service to the public, the FTC regulations apply. As FTC explains it, if you have a website that offers individual customers an online service to collect their health information and you sign a HIPAA business associate agreement with an insurance company to maintain the electronic health records of its customers, if a data breach occurs that affects all your users, "both the FTC Rule and HHS Rule would apply [18]."

A 2013 administrative complaint filed by the FTC against Atlanta-based LabMD will give you some sense of the Commission's enforcement actions in the healthcare arena. The lab's spreadsheet, which contained insurance billing details for several patients, was found on a public peer-to-peer file-sharing network. This exposed social security numbers, dates of birth, and health insurance information for more than 9000 individuals. The spreadsheet also contained standardized medical treatment codes. The FTC says that LabMD documents were also in the possession of identity thieves [19]. FTC says the lab "violated the FTC Act by engaging in unfair acts or practices due to its failure to prevent unauthorized access to patient information." LabMD challenged the Commission's decision, claiming that it had no authority to regulate PHI, but as of Jan. 22, 2015, the 11th Circuit Court dismissed the challenge to the enforcement action [20].

FTC and OCR joined forces in 2010 to file a complaint against the Rite Aid Pharmacy chain. The company agreed to pay $1 million to resolve the HHS allegations that it did not do enough to protect customers' PHI. FTC started its investigation after news reports surfaced stating that some of the pharmacies were discarding pharmacy labels and job applications in dumpsters that could be accessed by the public. The FTC settlement order required Rite Aid to "obtain, every two years for the next 20 years, an audit from a qualified, independent, third-party professional to ensure that its security program meets the standards of the order." The order required the chain to establish a comprehensive information security program [21].

DO NOT FORGET STATE LAWS

In addition to adhering to federal regulations, decision makers need to familiarize themselves with state laws that govern patient privacy and data security. The HIPAA Privacy Rule preempts state laws but there are a few exceptions. If, for example, a state law governing individually identifiable health information provides *greater* protection than the HIPAA rule, then the state's requirements take precedence [22].

It is also worth mentioning that the federal government is encouraging state attorneys general to pursue action against healthcare organizations that compromise PHI. In fact, HHS has provided training materials to help state AGs to investigate such claims.

To date, 47 states, plus the District of Columbia, Guam, Puerto Rico, and the Virgin Islands have laws that require private and government organizations to inform individuals if there is a security breach that compromises their personally identifiable information. Alabama, New Mexico, and South Dakota are the only states without such laws. A list of all the states with privacy laws, along with links to the statutes themselves, is available from the National Conference of State Legislatures on its web site [23]. And a detailed chart that outlines each state's data security breach notification law is also available online [24].

A detailed discussion of each state's privacy laws is beyond the scope of this book, but a few highlights are worth mentioning. As the Obama Administration and Congress consider stronger national legislature to improve cybersecurity, several states have recently taken steps to build stronger safeguards on their own. New Jersey, for instance, has passed a law requiring health insurers in the state to encrypt the personal information of policy holders or make that data unreadable, undecipherable, or unusable to anyone who should not have access to it. Montana has amended its breach notification law, expanding its definition of personal information to include medical record information. And the state of Washington has enacted a law that makes a failure to notify consumers of a data breach a violation of the state's Consumer Protection Act. Clearly, these and related state initiative mean healthcare providers have to be more vigilant than ever to prevent breaches and report them to all the appropriate authorities [25].

References

[1] J. Akers, R. Beckman. Violation or breach? Identifying, investigating, and reporting HIPAA incidents. https://www.datafiletechnologies.com/hipaa-violation-breach/#.VVsxYPlViko, 2013.

[2] Department of Health and Human Services. Protected health information. http://www.hhs.gov/ocr/privacy/hipaa/understanding/training/udmn.pdf.

[3] HHS NIH 2. Department of Health and Human Services National Institutes of Health, How can covered entities use and disclose protected health information for research and comply with the privacy rule? http://privacyruleandresearch.nih.gov/pr_08.asp.

[4] R. Herold, K. Beaver, The Practical Guide to HIPAA Privacy and Security Compliance, CRC Press, Boca Raton, (2015) 16-L 17.

[5] HHS.gov. Health information privacy, guidance regarding methods for de-identification of protected health information in accordance with the Health Insurance Portability and Accountability Act (HIPAA) Privacy Rule. http://www.hhs.gov/ocr/privacy/hipaa/understanding/coveredentities/De-identification/guidance.html.

[6] Anthem. How to access and sign up for identity theft repair and credit monitoring services. https://www.anthemfacts.com/.

[7] E. Weise. Anthem fined $1.7 million in 2010 breach. USA Today. http://www.usatoday.com/story/tech/2015/02/05/anthem-health-care-computer-security-breach-fine-17-million/22931345/, 2015.

[8] Department of Health and Human Services National Institutes of Health. To whom does the privacy rule apply and whom will it affect? http://privacyruleandresearch.nih.gov/pr_06.asp.

[9] HIPAA Office of Civil Rights (OCR). The HIPAA Privacy Rule's Right of Access and Health Information Technology. http://www.hhs.gov/ocr/privacy/hipaa/understanding/special/healthit/eaccess.pdf.

[10] HHS.gov. Does the HIPAA Privacy Rule permit a doctor, laboratory, or other health care provider to share patient health information for treatment purposes by fax, e-mail, or over the phone? http://www.hhs.gov/ocr/privacy/hipaa/faq/disclosures/482.html.

[11] Department of Health and Human Services Office of Civil Rights. Breach portal, customized search. https://ocrportal.hhs.gov/ocr/breach/breach_report.jsf;jsessionid=E1FDCA77CE8AB0D5D8FB57C9D246E51A.ajp13w.

[12] A.W. Latner. Fax sent to wrong number results in HIPAA violation, Renal and Urology News. http://www.renalandurologynews.com/hipaa-violation-wrong-fax-sent-physician-privacy/article/305022/, 2013.

[13] American Medical Association. Frequently asked questions about HIPAA. http://www.ama-assn.org/ama/pub/physician-resources/solutions-managing-your-practice/coding-billing-insurance/hipaahealth-insurance-portability-accountability-act/frequently-asked-questions.page.

[14] HHS.gov. Summary of HIPAA Privacy Rule: enforcement and penalties for noncompliance. http://www.hhs.gov/ocr/privacy/hipaa/understanding/summary/index.html.

[15] HHS.gov. Summary of HIPAA Security Rule. http://www.hhs.gov/ocr/privacy/hipaa/understanding/srsummary.html.

[16] HHS.gov. Breach Notification Rule. http://www.hhs.gov/ocr/privacy/hipaa/administrative/breachnotificationrule/index.html.

[17] Federal Trade Commission. Health Breach Notification Rule. https://www.ftc.gov/tips-advice/business-center/guidance/health-breach-notification-rule.

[18] Federal Trade Commission. Complying with the FTC's Health Breach Notification Rule. https://www.ftc.gov/tips-advice/business-center/guidance/complying-ftcs-health-breach-notification-rule.

[19] FTC 3. Federal Trade Commission. FTC files data security complaint against LabMD. https://www.ftc.gov/news-events/blogs/business-blog/2013/08/ftc-files-data-security-complaint-against-labmd, 2013.

[20] National Law Review. 11th circuit allows FTC Data Breach Case against LABMD to proceed. http://www.natlawreview.com/article/11th-circuit-allows-ftc-data-breach-case-against-labmd-to-proceed, 2015.

[21] Federal Trade Commission. Rite aid settles FTC charges that it failed to protect medical and financial privacy of customers and employees. https://www.ftc.gov/news-events/press-releases/2010/07/rite-aid-settles-ftc-charges-it-failed-protect-medical-and, 2010.

[22] HHS.gov. Does the HIPAA Privacy Rule preempt State laws? http://www.hhs.gov/ocr/privacy/hipaa/faq/preemption_of_state_law/399.html.

[23] National Conference of State Legislatures. Security Breach Notification Laws. http://www.ncsl.org/research/telecommunications-and-information-technology/security-breach-notification-laws.aspx, 2015.

[24] Mintz Levin. State data security breach notification laws. http://www.privacyandsecuritymatters.com/files/2015/01/state-data-breach-matrix-2015.pdf.

[25] MintzLevin. Privacy and security matters, State data breach notification law updates. http://www.privacyandsecuritymatters.com/2015/03/state-data-breach-notification-law-updates/, 2015.

CHAPTER 4

Risk Analysis

Before you can fix a problem, you have to measure it. You have probably heard that adage applied to business and to medicine many times. It is precisely the wisdom behind security risk analysis.

Before you can put security and privacy safeguards in place, your organization needs to start measuring things: Exactly how many servers, desktop computers, tablets, smartphones, laptops, external drives, thumb drives, photocopiers, fax machines, and so on are you responsible for? Where are they located? Which ones have protected health information (PHI) on them or have access to it? Do these devices move around your organization, changing users randomly? How vulnerable is each one of them to a data breach? How will they be discarded when no longer of use? Without a thorough inventory of these assets, it is almost impossible to protect the patient information they contain.

But before you start making measurements, you need to become familiar with the language of risk analysis. In healthcare, as in many other fields, the terms to understand include vulnerability, threat,, risk, incident, violation, and breach. They have specific connotations in the IT world, and without having an appreciation for the jargon, it will be that much harder to comply with the myriad government regulations—since the regulations usually incorporate the same language as the technology geeks who manage the data.

LEARNING THE JARGON

Executives may not feel comfortable admitting their ignorance to those who report to them, but that discomfort often turns to frustration when the experts they reach out to for help offer explanations couched in obscure terms—or use common terms in unfamiliar ways. With that in mind, here are some everyday terms that take on specific meaning in the context of healthcare security:

Vulnerability

To estimate the probability that various threats will compromise your system, you have to identify the unique vulnerabilities—or weaknesses—that exist in your individual organization. Those weaknesses will vary widely depending on what kind of safeguards you have already put in place. A poorly managed mobile device, for example, can make your computer network vulnerable if it does not contain anti-malware software, if the software is not regularly updated, if PHI resides on the device's unencrypted hard drive, or if your physicians are careless about leaving it out in the open for anyone to steal.

Threat Versus Risk

If you look up the word threat in a dictionary, you will find the word risk listed as one of its synonyms, but in the world of information security, they are not synonymous. A threat in this context is something that has the potential to cause harm to your IT system or to patient information. Malware, phishing schemes, and hackers are threats. So are power outages, hurricanes, fires, and floods.

A risk, on the other hand, is the likelihood or probability that such threats will actually compromise your computer system, or in some other way deprive patients of their information, or expose it to unauthorized individuals. Security specialists Rebecca Herold and Kevin Beaver offer a concise definition, referring to a risk as "The likelihood that the confidentiality, integrity, or availability of PHI will be adversely affected if a threat exploits a vulnerability" [1].

Another set of terms that have specific meaning in healthcare security are incident, violation, and breach. A security/privacy incident usually refers to some action or event that does not comply with your *organization's* policies and procedures, whereas a violation usually refers to an incident that is not compliant with government regulations. Finally a breach refers to a violation that exposes PHI.

A medical practice or hospital commits a HIPAA violation if, for example, it fails to provide patients with a privacy notice. But it commits a data breach if it allows an unauthorized person to gain access to PHI. Unfortunately the English language is rather slippery, so as you listen to "security speak," keep in mind that a breach is also a violation. And an incident can be a violation.

COMPLIANCE VERSUS MANAGEMENT

As you consider the risk analysis process, it is important to appreciate the difference between compliance and management. Both are essential but neither is enough on their own. Both HIPAA and the HITECH Act require you to *comply* with a set of regulations that include a security risk analysis. The HIPAA Security Rule states that an organization must: "Conduct an accurate and thorough assessment of the potential risks and vulnerabilities to the confidentiality, integrity, and availability of electronic PHI (ePHI) held by the covered entity." That rule is spelled out in 45 CFR 164.308. (CFR refers to the Code of Federal Regulations, which includes 50 titles. Title 45 is the section that covers public welfare.) The Meaningful Use program, which also requires a security risk analysis, refers applicants back to the same HIPAA regulation.

Either security analysis must be a formal process that is fully documented and safely saved. Said documentation has to be available to government auditors when they come calling. And by all indications, they will. The Centers for Medicare and Medicaid Services (CMS) is auditing healthcare providers to make sure they have done a risk analysis. Many practices and hospitals have already been audited to confirm that they qualified for the Meaningful Use incentive dollars they received. And other federal auditors will be coming to visit to confirm that you meet HIPAA regulations independent of the MU program.

The statistics on CMS audits change daily but a recent tally compiled by Health Security Solutions found that among the 3820 prepayment audits the agency had conducted, about 21% had failed the Meaningful Use audit. Among the 4601 postpayment audits of eligible clinicians that CMS performed, 24% failed to meet MU standards. Health Security Solutions estimated that the average incentive payment these providers will likely have to return is around $17,000. Among hospitals that enrolled in the MU program, about 600 had been through a postpayment audit and 4.7% had failed. It was estimated that they will have to return between approximately $280,000 and $3.4 million each [2].

Although compliance with the regulations is a critical part of an organization's responsibility, it is not enough. Risk management requires a different mindset, appreciating not just the letter of the law but its spirit. By way of analogy, if you drive your car through a town with a 30 mph speed limit, you comply with that speed limit because you do not want a speeding ticket. But if you appreciate the spirit of the law, you also slow down because you realize that at 30 mph, you are less likely to kill your neighbor's son when he runs out into the street to retrieve his basketball.

Similarly, most decision makers in healthcare organizations realize that complying with HIPAA can save them from fines, lawsuits, and loss of reputation. But those with a management mindset appreciate the fact that going beyond the bare minimum to protect patients' information can prevent a variety of nightmares for the many patients they serve. Creating a robust risk management program protects patients from having to cope with the problems that result from having their personal or medical identities stolen, whether that means being denied a mortgage because their credit rating has plummeted, or being ostracized when their employer and coworkers learn of their HIV status. It is not unrealistic to imagine a scenario in which one of your patients has his medical identity stolen, he enters the ER with an infected appendix and the nurse says: "Mr. Peterson, you already had an appendectomy two weeks ago. You can't have more than one appendix."

Such scenarios are not that far-fetched given a recent Ponemon survey on medical identity theft, which found that 65% of the victims of medical ID theft had to pay on average $13,450 per person to medical providers, insurance plans, legal counsel, and others [3]. The same survey suggested that about half of all consumers would "find another healthcare provider if they were concerned about the security of their medical records" [4]. Statistics such as these leave little doubt that taking a casual view toward security risk assessment can have financial consequence for any healthcare organization.

Of course, even the most conscientious risk management mentality has to have limitations since you also have a financial obligation to employees and other stakeholders. You have to set risk priorities and spend your security dollars wisely. As John Halamka, MD, chief information officer at Beth Israel Deaconess Medical Center in Boston, explains it in his book *GeekDoctor*: "Do you consider the HIV status of patients to be the same security priority as protecting the data integrity of the library catalog? Probably not" [5]. With that in mind, the analysis will require you to stratify your risks and put your most sensitive assets behind the strongest walls.

So how exactly does a practice, hospital, insurer, or business associate move beyond a compliance mindset and create a robust security management system? The Office of the National Coordinator for Health Information Technology (ONC), which is a division of the U.S. Department of Health and Human Services (HHS), recently issued a guide to privacy and security of electronic health information that outlines a 7-step approach to security management that includes a risk analysis but is not limited to it [6]. It is worth considering if you want to move beyond the "let's avoid the speeding ticket" mindset.

THE ONC APPROACH TO RISK ANALYSIS AND SECURITY MANAGEMENT

ONC suggests healthcare providers consider these 7 steps—but does not mandate this approach:

- Lead your culture, select your team, and learn
- Document your process, findings, and actions
- Review existing security of ePHI (perform security risk analysis)
- Develop an action plan
- Manage and mitigate risks

- Attest for meaningful use security-related objective
- Monitor, audit, and update security on an ongoing basis

Step 1

For many practices and hospitals, the first step is usually the hardest because reshaping the workplace culture is challenging, especially in medicine, which is conservative and often resistant to change. Promoting a culture that truly sees the value of protecting patient privacy and security can also prove difficult for another reason: Making PHI more secure often means making it harder not just for unauthorized persons to get to the information but harder for clinicians as well. Tightening up policies on passwords, for instance, or locking out authorized users to an electronic health record 5 min after they walk away from the workstation can be inconvenient, especially in an ER, where the nature of the work requires clinicians to move around a lot. We will go into a more detailed discussion about creating a security conscious culture in chapter 8: Educating Medical and Administrative Staff.

Step 1 also involves the establishment of a team that has oversight of the risk analysis, as well as other aspects of your security initiative. ONC also recommends choosing a security officer, discussing your security needs with the EHR vendor, reading up on the HIPAA rules, and perhaps bringing in a qualified professional to help conduct the risk analysis—if there is no one on your team capable of handling the responsibility. If you decide to bring in a third party, be certain that consultant has the right credentials. Both the Healthcare Information and Management Systems Society (HIMSS) and the American Health Information Management Association (AHIMA) have certification systems in place to help you determine who is and is not right for the job.

AHIMA bestows a stamp of approval referred to as CHPS, indicating that the person is Certified in Healthcare Privacy and Security. In addition to passing an exam, it also requires IT professionals to have a college degree and several years' experience working in the specialty. HIMSS offers the CPHIMS credentials, which means the person is a Certified Professional in Healthcare Information and Management Systems. HIMSS requires CPHIMS specialists to either have a bachelor's degree and at least 3 years of experience in healthcare IT or a graduate degree and two years in healthcare IT.

Step 2

Ask any healthcare attorney about documentation, and they will agree that it is essential in almost every aspect of patient care. No less so in managing security risks. In step 2, ONC suggests setting up a master folder in your computer system that contains all your security findings, decisions, and actions, along with a copy of the risk analysis itself.

Host Type	Risk	Examples of Mitigation Steps
Office-based EHRs	Natural disaster could greatly disrupt the availability of, and even destroy, ePHI.	Always store routine backups offsite.
Office-based EHRs	You directly control the security settings.	Regardless of your practice size, follow best practices on policies and procedures about access to ePHI. For example, use password controls and automatic logout features.
Office-based EHRs	The security features on your office-based EHR may not be as up-to-date and sophisticated as an Internet-hosted EHR.	Maintain ongoing communication with your EHR developer about new features and their criticality to the security of the EHR.
Office-based EHRs	When public and private information security requirements change, you have to figure out how to update your EHR and work out any bugs.	Routinely monitor for changes in federal, state, or private-sector information security requirements and adjust settings as needed.
Internet-hosted (cloud-based) EHRs	You are more dependent on the reliability of your Internet connection. Your data may be stored outside the United States and other countries may have different health information privacy and security laws that may apply to such offshore data.	Confirm that your EHR host follows US security standards and requirements.
Internet-hosted (cloud-based) EHRs	The developer may control many security settings.	The adequacy of these settings may be hard to assess, but ask for specific information.
Internet-hosted (cloud-based) EHRs	In the future, the developer might request extra fees to update your EHR for compliance as federal, state, and private-sector information security requirements evolve.	Ensure your EHR stays compliant. Before you buy, it is OK to ask your developer about fees it may charge for security updates.

FIGURE 4.1 Examples of potential information security risks with different types of EHR hosts.
http://www.healthit.gov/sites/default/files/privacy-and-security-guide.pdf.

Step 3

This step in the ONC approach is the risk analysis itself. ONC suggests the use of the SRA tool, which will help small to middle size practices and which is discussed in more detail below. As you prepare this analysis, keep in mind that the risks of exposing PHI will differ in an office-based EHR versus and internet-hosted EHR. Fig. 4.1 illustrates some of the differences in security risks between the two types of EHRs.

Also keep in mind that government auditors will expect you to not only protect PHI in an EHR but in *every* other component of your record keeping systems. That means the practice management program, revenue cycle management system, as well as in any data in motion, for example, any emails, text messages, and files sent to Dropbox or other file sharing application. It also means protecting paper files, including their disposal. More than one healthcare organization has been fined for not following common sense precautions when discarding paper patient records.

Step 4

In this step, the action plan should be designed to mitigate the problems identified in the risk analysis, says ONC. Chapter 5: Reducing the Risk of a Data Breach will go into more depth on preventive strategies to mitigate the risk of a HIPAA violation or data breach, but ONC offers a helpful list of low-cost, highly effective measures that will get the action plan off the ground:

- Say "no" to staff requests to take home laptops containing unencrypted ePHI. (Some security specialists believe, however, that it is best to never say "no" but to say "Let's find a secure way to do what you want to do.")
- Remove hard drives from old computers before you get rid of them.
- Do not email ePHI unless you know the data is encrypted.
- Make sure your server is in a room accessible only to authorized staff, and keep the door locked.
- Make sure the entire office understands that passwords should not be shared or easy to guess.
- Notify your office staff that you are required to monitor their access randomly.
- Maintain a working fire extinguisher in case of fire.
- Check your EHR server often for viruses and malware.

As you put together your action plan, also consider some basic questions such as:

- Who has the keys to your practice? It may be necessary to change the physical locks and computer passwords when employees or contractors leave your practice if they still have access to patient information.
- Where, when, and how often do you back up? Do you have at least one backup kept offsite? Can your data be recovered from the backups? Remember, losing patient records will not only cripple your day-to-day functioning, it will also deprive patients of their information, which they are entitled to by law.
- What is your contingency/disaster plan when/if your server crashes and you cannot directly recover data?

The last item on the ONC list is especially important, namely: monitoring, auditing, and updating security on an ongoing basis. Some healthcare organizations have made the mistake of doing a detailed security risk analysis, tucking it away in their computer system and never giving it another thought for years. The HIPAA rule is very specific, however, in insisting that risk analysis must be an ongoing process. As new technology is incorporated into a practice or hospital, the potential for PHI to be compromised increases, requiring more advanced safeguards in some cases.

The Office of the National Coordinator for Health Information Technology is not the only group encouraging healthcare decision makers to replace their compliance mentality with a risk management approach. Gartner, one of the world's largest IT research and advisory companies, has been urging C-suite executives to make the switch as well. In its view, compliance is part of a much larger risk management program that balances the need to adhere to security regulations with the needs of the business as a whole. Two of Gartner's key recommendations are the following:

> "Create a formal and defensible program of controls based on the specific situation and risks unique to each organization.
> Build a formal program that can adapt to the changing landscape of regulatory requirements that also protects you from reasonably anticipated risks" [7].

Gartner point outs that the HIPAA regulations themselves encourage this shift from a compliance point of view to a broader risk management approach by instructing healthcare organizations to do a risk analysis and to put *reasonable* controls in place that take into account *reasonably anticipated* risks. A simple security checklist is not enough to make that paradigm shift. The IT research firm goes on to outline a detailed roadmap to help businesses move from reactive old school thinking about security through a 5-phase evolution that eventually arrives at a more sophisticated "adaptive" model. Said roadmap is illustrated on their web site [7].

FINDING THE RIGHT ANALYSIS TOOLS

There are several risk analysis tools available that will help you through the process. And since CMS does not prescribe a specific tool or outline specific instructions on how to conduct the analysis, you have to choose one that best suits your needs, depending on the size of your organization, the sophistication of your record keeping system, and the expertise of your staff.

Several toolkits, guidelines, and risk analysis vendors are worth considering. If you conclude that the risk analysis process is beyond the expertise of your staff, you can hire firms such as Coalfire, Principle Logic, or several other reputable vendors. For detailed guidelines on performing a risk analysis, the first source to review is the National Institute of Standards and Technology (NIST), part of the US Department of Commerce. NIST publishes *Guide for Conducting Risk Assessments* [8].

Herzig, Walsh, and Gallagher also describe a detailed risk analysis process in their guide to healthcare security [9]. Their approach includes (1) creating an inventory of applications and systems, (2) identifying threats, (3) determining what safeguards are currently in place to deal with those threats, (4) identifying vulnerabilities, and (5) estimating the likelihood that each threat will materialize. The remaining steps include an impact analysis, a risk determination that includes a numerical score, advice on how to mitigate the risks you spot, and a final documentation phase.

Their risk score plots the potential impact of a risk against the likelihood of it occurring to generate a number from 1 to 9—referred to as the OCTAVE approach—which can then be used to help you determine how much time and resources you want to devote to fixing the problem.

As I have mentioned previously, HHS and the Office of Civil Rights place a great deal of emphasis on documenting the results of your risk analysis. Herzig et al's recommendations on the final documentation are worth a closer look. They suggest creating three types of documents: Risk profiles, a risk analysis report, and a risk remediation report. One especially valuable feature of their risk analysis report is its mitigate/transfer/accept option. This lets the organization make a list of potential safeguards or "controls," designate the amount of resources needed to put them in place, and decide whether to install the control (ie, *mitigate* the risk), pass on the responsibility to someone else (eg, *transfer* the risk to a cybersecurity insurance firm for example), or just *accept* the risk without doing anything.

The purpose of these documents, as well as those generated by several other risk analysis tools, is to prove to government auditors that you have taken your responsibility to protect patient information seriously and have made a *reasonable* effort to adhere to the HIPAA privacy and security rules. The authorities do not expect you to create an impenetrable fortress, but neither do they want a simple checklist completed.

HIMSS also provides resources to help providers perform a risk analysis [10]. Its risk assessment toolkit includes white papers, best practices, and a variety of other resources to help providers manage the process. I have featured one of its tools below, which uses the example of a small medical practice to keep things simple. Also keep in mind that the description given subsequently only covers a portion of the assessment process. Since the primary audience for this book is executives and other decision makers and not security specialists or compliance officers, my purpose is not to provide a detailed how-to guide but a general overview that will allow you to provide direction to those who are responsible for actually doing the analysis.

HIMSS provides the tool/sample analysis as an Excel file and assumes the practice has five employees, including a physician, biller, nurse—who doubles as practice manager—and two administrative assistants. It also assumes you have an in-house server with an EHR system and practice management software, as well as a cloud-based email system and a laptop to run EKGs.

The sample analysis contains cells that allow the practice to plug in its threats and vulnerabilities, and the nature of the risk each vulnerability presents. It also asks you to estimate the risk level for each vulnerability as low, medium, or high, and requires you to list the likely impact of each threat and what existing safeguards are in place to prevent a mishap. So, for example, one of the vulnerabilities listed is a missing policy and procedures manual that outlines the practice's security plan. Without a manual, the practice has no clear cut direction from the physician owner defining best practices. That is a serious deficiency in the mind of any competent auditor.

One of the threats described in this Excel file is from an employee who wants to steal sensitive data or simply does not know enough about basic security to take reasonable precautions. Without specific policies that tell staffers not to write system passwords on Post-its that are pasted next to their workstations, for instance, the physician owner will be held responsible when a CMS auditor shows up and spots this obvious mistake.

Similarly, without a written policy that instructs staffers not to click on hyperlinks in suspicious emails, it is that much easier for an outsider to trick them into logging into a malicious web site that can track their keystrokes or plant some other type of malware on your server.

Another vulnerability in the HIMSS sample risk analysis is described as: "Unauthorized access of data transmitted over the Internet (eg, remote access use by employees/contractors or transmitting data to business associates)". In this sample analysis, the likelihood of a data breach resulting from this specific vulnerability is listed as low because the practice was smart enough to only allow remote access to its server through an encrypted virtual private network or VPN. It also explains that transmissions from their business associate use a secure socket layer or SSL encrypted web browser.

Speaking of business associates, in 2013, HHS updated the privacy and security protections originally incorporated in HIPAA, which was introduced in 1996. Back then, the primary focus had been on medical practices, hospitals, health plans, and a variety of health professionals. The more recent Omnibus Rule, which is based on statutory changes under the HITECH Act, put a great deal more emphasis on the responsibilities of vendors, contractors, and subcontractors working with these organizations and clinicians. These business associates (BAs) are now required to do a risk analysis as well, and healthcare organizations have to take into account their relationships with their BAs when they do their own risk analysis, as you will learn subsequently.

TAPPING THE HHS RESOURCES

ONC, working together with the HHS Office of Civil Rights and the HHS Office of General Counsel, also offers some useful advice and tools to help your organization conduct a risk analysis. Like most other expert sources, ONC points out that doing a risk analysis properly takes a great deal of time and effort.

They have created a security risk assessment application called SRA Tool that is available at www.healthit.gov [11]. You can download an executable file containing the program onto a Windows computer or iPad; it works like any other desktop application. Or you can download three Word documents that divide the questions into the three categories, namely administrative, technical, and physical safeguards.

Assuming for the moment that you have the SRA Tool loaded on a Windows computer, the program walks you through check boxes to help you assess your security system's strengths and weaknesses.

Although the SRA Tool does not require you to be intimately acquainted with the long list of HIPAA security regulations, working your way through the analysis tool will make more sense if you have a basic understanding of how the government has structured these rules. If you are not a lawyer, your eyes would probably glaze over if you had to read through the *Federal Register* explanation of the regulations. But a broad overview is bearable.

The regulations related to healthcare privacy and security have the cryptic label 45.CFR Section164. As I mentioned earlier, CFR refers to the Code of Federal Regulations, which includes 50 titles. Title 45 is the section that covers public welfare. And within that section are the regulations that pertain to the Department of Health and Human Services (Subtitle A). Within Subtitle A is subchapter C, which covers security and privacy. Subpart C of Subchapter C covers the security standards for protecting ePHI. Subpart D covers notification requirements in case of a data breach, and Subpart E covers the privacy of individually identifiable health information. All three subparts are listed as Section 164. So, for instance, the regulations on protecting ePHI are 45.CFR Section 164.302 to 45.CFR Section 164.318 [12]. (More detail on these regulations are located in the Cornell University Law School's Legal Information Institute web site.)

With a basic grasp of how the regulations are structured, let's take a look at the SRA tool in action, bearing in mind that the administrative regulations are covered in Sections 164.308, 164.314, and 164.316. The technical regulations are in Section 164.312, and the physical regulations are in Section 164.310.

Fig. 4.2 is a screen capture of the graphic user interface in the SRA tool, with the first administrative question—§164.308(a)(1)(i)—displayed in the upper left hand portion of the screen.

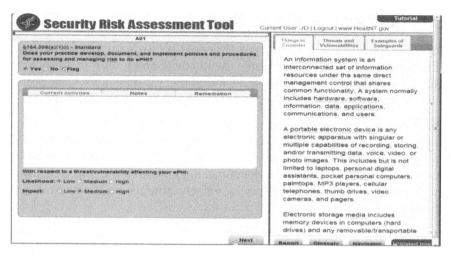

FIGURE 4.2 A sample page from the Security Risk Assessment Tool.

As you answer each question and click through to the next one, the program saves your answer, inserting it into a report. Here are a few sample questions from each of the three categories:

Administrative:

- Does your practice develop, document, and implement policies and procedures for assessing and managing risk to its ePHI?
- Does your practice have a process for periodically reviewing its risk analysis policies and procedures and making updates as necessary?
- Does your practice categorize its information systems on the basis of the potential impact to your practice should they become unavailable?

Technical:

- Does your practice activate an automatic logoff that terminates an electronic session after a predetermined period of user inactivity?
- Does your practice use the evaluation from its risk analysis to help determine the frequency and scope of its audits, when identifying the activities that will be tracked?
- Does your practice analyze the activities performed by all of its workforce and service providers to identify the extent to which each needs access to ePHI?

Physical:

- Do you have an inventory of the physical systems, devices, and media in your office space that are used to store or contain ePHI?

- Do you have policies and procedures for the physical protection of your facilities and equipment? This includes controlling the environment inside the facility.
- Do you have policies and procedures for the physical protection of your facilities and equipment? This includes controlling the environment inside the facility.

Before you can start answering these questions, you will want to familiarize yourself with four tabs marked Users, About Your Practice, Business Associates, and Asset Inventory. (They are not shown in the screen capture here, but are visible earlier in the analysis process.) Once you create a user name, you add your practice's demographics, and then add the names of all your business associates, each in a separate field. The Asset Inventory allows you to create individual fields for an EHR, practice management system, photocopier—which can store patient data—and any other relevant practice asset.

The application even provides a box for "assignee," which lets you document who in your organization is responsible for each asset that contains, receives, and/or transmits ePHI. You can already see that the tool is creating an accountability trail for you and your staff. If an Office of Civil Rights auditor comes calling, you can present the final report to prove you have done your due diligence. But also keep in mind that if you have a data breach, this documentation can also serve as an indictment, pointing a finger at those who were supposed to be responsible for safeguarding each asset.

After you have filled out these initial fields and read the explanatory text about administrative, technical, and physical safeguards, you click a "Start Assessment" button to begin the actual analysis process. That is when you will see the screen that is depicted in the screen capture shown previously.

BEWARE THE "REQUIRED" VERSUS "ADDRESSABLE" CONFUSION

The SRA tool will tell you whether the question being displayed on the screen refers to a "required" or "addressable" implementation specification. The difference between addressable and required gets some healthcare providers in trouble because they mistakenly assume that addressable HIPAA regulations are optional. A better understanding of the regulatory language should clear up any misunderstandings.

A required implementation specification is self-explanatory. HHS says: "The concept of "addressable implementation specifications" was developed to provide [healthcare organizations] additional flexibility with respect to compliance with the security standards. In meeting standards that contain addressable implementation specifications, a [healthcare organization] will do one of the following for each addressable specification:

a. Implement the addressable implementation specifications
b. Implement one or more alternative security measures to accomplish the same purpose
c. Not implement either an addressable implementation specification or an alternative" [13].

HHS goes on to explain that you have to put an addressable implementation specification in place if "it is reasonable and appropriate to do so."

If your risk analysis concludes that it is not reasonable and appropriate to put a certain security control in place, you are expected to find an equivalent alternative. The agency further states that the decision to put a certain safeguard in place or choose an equally effective alternative will depend on a variety of factors, including your risk mitigation strategy, what security measures are already in place, and the cost of implementation. And if you choose option C from the above list because you believe you have justification, you still need to meet the *standard* upon which the implementation specification was based, as spelled out in the HIPAA regulations. Whatever decision you make, the decision, as well as the rationale, needs to be documented in writing.

Admittedly this can all get confusing without a concrete example. Let's use HIPAA regulation 164.312(e)(1) to illustrate the point. "Transmission security" is the standard that has to be met. The regulation lists encryption as one of the addressable implementation specifications. So if you are transmitting patient information to another medical practice, for example, and your means of transmission is encrypted, you have met the standard using the recommended implementation specification. In other words, you have chosen option A.

However, if your organization has another secure method of transmitting PHI, it can be substituted as an alternative, assuming you provide good reason for doing so and you document that reason. If you decide, however, that neither an encrypted email system, nor any other measure is necessary and you choose option C, you better have a very good reason to justify that decision, keeping in mind that you *must* still meet the standard, which is "transmission security." I am hard pressed to imagine a good reason for choosing option C in this scenario.

Similarly there is a HIPAA standard referred to as "Access control" and one of the addressable specifications to meet that standard is encryption and decryption. Typically that would include encrypting any data on a laptop, or the hard drive itself. Officially, however, since this is an addressable standard, you are not required to encrypt a laptop containing PHI; but given the fact that there are so many healthcare providers who have had to pay large fines for losing laptops that were not encrypted, it is hard to imagine a viable alternative to encryption that would convince auditors.

Here is a second example: You are a provider that stores all its PHI on servers that are physically protected in a data center. The data are transmitted within the organization over a private network. You may decide that the access control standard that suggests encryption as a safeguard is unreasonable in this setting, in which case your risk analysis would conclude that the data does not need to be further protected for storage or for internal transmission. Your equivalent alternative in this case—option B—is "physical protection."

Security specialists Rebecca Herold and Kevin Beaver sum up the best approach to handling addressable implementation specifications, stating that covered entities "should consider treating every implementation specification as if it is required yet scalable and flexible. The time spent trying to determine whether or not something should be implemented based on the results of a risk analysis may very well be more difficult than implementing the specification itself" [14].

MOVING BEYOND A CHECKLIST OF SECURITY QUESTIONS

With an understanding of the distinction between required and addressable specs, you are prepared to take advantage of several other SRA Tool features. As you work your way through the analysis, you will see that it is so much more than a checklist of questions. The tabs to the right of each question are labeled "Things to Consider, Threats and Vulnerabilities, and Examples of Safeguards." That last tab will point you to suggestions on some of the ways you can mitigate the threats and vulnerabilities alluded to in each question. The information provided in these three sections are especially valuable for clinicians who do not have an in-depth knowledge of technology and security.

If you are a decision maker responsible for delegating specific security tasks to others in your practice, the "Flag" check box below each question allows you to call attention to a question that requires additional action or to indicate to someone on staff that they need to review or answer the question. A "remediation" section under each question provides space for you to explain what is being done to fix any security gaps—an especially important piece of documentation in the HIPAA universe.

As with other risk analysis tools, SRA Tool asks you to rate the likelihood that a particular threat can affect your ePHI by choosing a low, medium, or high score.

Similarly you can rate the impact if the regulation referred to in the question is not met. Give careful thought to how you use these six radio buttons since your assessment of the likelihood and impact of each threat/vulnerability will be used down the road to decide where you will use your resources and spend your money as you figure out which security gaps need attention and which can be ignored.

Once you and your colleagues have finished the analysis, you can view the analysis report as a simple chart within the SRA tool, convert it to a pdf file, or export it to Microsoft Excel. You can also view an interim version of the report before you finish all 156 questions. There is also a navigator button that will take you to a list of all the questions you have completed to date. And since the process of completing this analysis can get exhausting, you can quit the program and come back at another time to finish. But do not forget to log out rather than just closing the application.

Since the Omnibus Security rule has been put into effect, the security status of a healthcare provider's business associates has taken center stage. If you ignore their role in protecting patient data, you will share the blame if a data breach can be traced to a BA's negligence. With that in mind, the SRA tool will help you assess the role of BAs. Here are some of the questions it poses:

Does your practice know all business associates and the access that each requires for your practice's facilities, information systems, electronic devices, and ePHI?

Do you have a Facility User Access List of workforce members, business associates, and others who are authorized to access your facilities where ePHI and related information systems are located? As HHS points on, having a list of BAs who are permitted to enter your facility is an important part of the risk analysis, not only because you do not want imposters entering your buildings, but because you need to keep out any business associate who has been terminated or transferred.

Once you have worked your way through all the questions in the SRA tool and generated a final report, you will not send it to HHS. It is for your internal use only. And the government is quick to point out that completion of the analysis does not guarantee compliance with any federal, state, or local laws, nor is it an exhaustive or definitive source of information on healthcare security and privacy. But on a more positive note, HHS states: "The application, available for downloading at www.HealthIT.gov/security-risk-assessment also produces a report that can be provided to auditors" [15].

If you decide to use the SRA tool to do your security analysis, keep in mind that the process can get quite tedious and requires a lot of patience. The tool is not as intuitive as it can be, so the best way to survive the analysis is to first view the 9.5 min video that explains how to navigate the application [16]. HHS also provides a text-based user guide, also located on the healthit.gov site [17].

As you contemplate which security risk analysis tool to use or consider hiring a third party to walk you through the risk-analysis process, there is one miscalculation you do not want to make: Do not be fooled into thinking that your practice or business is too small to require a risk analysis. HHS has published a list of 10 risk analysis myths that should be required reading for healthcare organizations large and small. At the top of the list is the mistaken notion that a risk analysis is *optional*. It is not. The list includes several other myths: simply installing a certified EHR system is all that is needed to meet the government's requirement to perform a risk analysis; my EHR vendor will take care of the risk analysis if I install his system; the risk analysis only needs to look at the EHR. Falling victim to any of these myths can get quite expensive (Fig. 4.2).

References

[1] R. Herold, K. Beaver, The Practical Guide to HIPAA Privacy and Security Compliance, second ed, CRC Press, Boca Raton, (2015) p. 233.

[2] Health Security Solutions. Meaningful use audits infographic. http://www.healthsecuritysolutions.com/2014/11/05/meaningful-use-audits-infographic/, 2014.

[3] S. Peters. Medical identity theft costs victims $13,450 apiece, *Information Week Dark Reading*. http://www.darkreading.com/medical-identity-theft-costs-victims-$13450-apiece/d/d-id/1319210, 2015.

[4] E. McCann. Medical identity theft hits all-time high, Healthcare IT News. http://www.healthcareitnews.com/news/medical-identity-theft-hits-all-time-high?mkt_tok=3RkMMJWWfF9ws RogvKrOZKXonjHpfsX56egsWKS1lMI%2F0ER3fOvrPUfGjI4GTsFnI%2BSLDwEYGJlv6SgFQ 7LHMbpszbgPUhM%3D, 2015.

[5] J. Halamka, GeekDoctor: Life as a Healthcare CIO, Healthcare Information and Management Society (HIMSS), Chicago, Ill, (2014) p. 142.

[6] Office of the National Coordinator for Health Information Technology. Guide to Privacy and Security of Electronic Health Information, Version 2.0. http://www.healthit.gov/sites/default/files/privacy-and-security-guide.pdf, 2015.

[7] P. Proctor, J. Wheeler. Compliance is no longer a primary driver for IT risk and security. Gartner. http://www.gartner.com/technology/reprints.do?id=1-2G75KQX&ct=150520&st=sb, 2013.

[8] R.S. Ross. Guide for conducting risk assessments, NIST SP - 800-30 Rev 1. http://www.nist.gov/manuscript-publication-search.cfm?pub_id=912091, 2012.

[9] T.W. Herzig, T. Walsh, L.A. Gallagher, Implementing Information Security in Healthcare: Building a Security Program, Healthcare Information and Management Systems Society, Chicago, IL, (2013).

[10] HIMSS Resource Library. Sample risk assessment for a physician practice. http://www.himss.org/ResourceLibrary/ResourceDetail.aspx?ItemNumber=21449, 2013.

[11] HealthIT.gov. Security risk assessment, What is the security risk assessment tool (SRA tool)? http://www.healthit.gov/providers-professionals/security-risk-assessment-tool.

[12] Cornell University Law School. 45 CFR 164.308 - Administrative safeguards. https://www.law.cornell.edu/cfr/text/45/164.308.

[13] HHS.gov. What is the difference between addressable and required implementation specifications in the Security Rule? http://www.hhs.gov/ocr/privacy/hipaa/faq/securityrule/2020.html.

[14] R. Herold, K. Beaver, The Practical Guide to HIPAA Privacy and Security Compliance, second ed, CRC Press, Boca Raton, (2015) p. 213.

[15] HHS.gov. HHS releases security risk assessment tool to help providers with HIPAA compliance. http://www.hhs.gov/news/press/2014pres/03/20140328a.html, 2014.

[16] HealthIT.gov. Security risk assessment videos, How can I learn more before getting started? http://www.healthit.gov/providers-professionals/security-risk-assessment-videos.

[17] The Office of the National Coordinator for Health Information Technology (ONC). Security risk assessment (SRA) tool user guide. http://www.healthit.gov/sites/default/files/risk_assessment_user_guide_final_3_26_2014.pdf, 2014.

CHAPTER 5

Reducing the Risk of a Data Breach

Healthcare organizations are slowly starting to get the message that they need to take cybersecurity more seriously and are *slowly* investing more resources in this area. But many providers and their business associates still underestimate the dollars and cents needed to adequately protect patient information. According to Larry Ponemon, a well-respected analyst in healthcare security, "The average Fortune 500 company budgets $44 million a year for security, including networking and all other aspects... (Most) hospitals have less than a million to budget on cyber security." [1] And although data breaches at large corporations such as Target and Home Depot still get most of the media attention, a growing number of cyber thieves are seeing the value of medical data.

Many clinicians and hospitals are more inclined to invest in a new MRI machine than update their computer operating system, install encryption software, or put a robust employee training program in place to instill a security conscious culture. Granted, a new imaging device may encourage more patient referrals and generate significant revenue, but as chapter 2: How Well-Protected is Your Protected Health Information? Perception Versus Reality explained, few patients are going to come into the clinic or hospital if they fear their medical identity is going to be stolen. And experiencing a large breach of patient data will probably get you the kind of publicity that drives patients away.

Just how valuable is a patient's medical identity on the black market? Estimates vary between $6 and 50 per record, with some researchers suggesting it is far more valuable than credit card numbers. Thieves have been known to use medical identity information to submit fraudulent bills to Medicare, fill prescriptions for narcotics, buy medical equipment, and have expensive procedures done, leaving others with the bill.

If you have performed the security risk analysis described in the last chapter, your organization is in a much better position to prevent a PHI breach, along with the potential for medical identity theft that accompanies such breaches. The purpose of this chapter is to go into a more detailed approach to safeguarding PHI.

SEEING THE LARGER PICTURE

There is a long list of technological tools that can help healthcare organizations protect patient information, including encryption, user authentication, mobile device management software, firewalls, and antimalware programs, but an effective preventive strategy requires a more holistic perspective. As Tom Walsh, a veteran security specialist, once explained it, any attempt to strengthen one's defenses requires you look at three important areas of concern: people, processes, and technology [2].

Your weakest link is always people, those troublesome "carbon-based interface units" as Walsh calls them. Several large-scale data breaches have been traced to employees being duped by various phishing scams, for example. During these scams, employees click on an email attachment from a "friend" or other seemingly trustworthy source, only to be sent to a web site that loads malware onto the individual's computer or network the employee works on. One of the most effective ways to block such intrusions is by educating your physicians, nurses, administrators, business associates, and anyone else who has access to patient data.

The people problem can manifest itself in other ways as well. If you put in place security procedures that make it too difficult for clinicians to provide quality patient care, they are probably going to rebel, or look for workarounds that are less secure. Clinicians may need to compromise and accept a measure of inconvenience in order to make their online activity more secure, but by the same token, security measures need to meet a reasonable standard, and they need to be understandable to the clinicians and administrative staff who use them. That once again requires well-thought out employee training and a set of sensible policies and procedures that are distributed to everyone in the organization.

THE BEST MINDSET: GUILTY UNTIL PROVEN INNOCENT

Since people are the weakest link in the security chain, let's start with them, and their vulnerability to email and Internet scams that use social engineering.

Social engineering essentially taps into many of the normal human personality traits that allow a society to function, traits like the desire to help out persons in need, the quest for recognition or financial gain, everyone's natural curiosity about their neighbors' affairs, just to name a few. Hackers rely on these tendencies to convince potential victims to open infected emails or web sites. A report from Trend Micro suggests that more than 90% of cyberattacks begin with such spear phishing emails [3].

Spear phishing refers to the targeted nature of the emails sent to potential victims. They may call you by name, mention your job title, or mention other personal information that email recipients assume can only originate with friends or business associates, or companies that you already have a relationship with. If a hacker has already infected one person's machine and gains access to their address book, he or she can then send phishing emails to those on that list. Since the intended new victim sees a friend's address, they often assume the message is legitimate.

There are so many ingenious ways to create a convincing phishing email that the best approach to preventing being duped is to assume that almost *every* message that arrives in your inbox is a scam until proven otherwise: guilty until proven innocent.

The most important piece of advice you can give staffers is: Do not click on hyperlinks embedded in an email, unless you are absolutely certain it is from a legitimate source. Unfortunately, many people do not believe that they would ever fall for such trickery. "I am too smart to be fooled by social engineering tricks." One way to convince them otherwise is by running a fake phishing scam.

Tom Cochran, formerly in charge of White House digital technology, was able to convince his coworkers at Atlanta Media that they were easy prey by sending out a fake phishing email to all the employees at the firm. Within 2 hours, he had his proof: "Almost half of the company opened the email, and 58% of those employees clicked the faux malicious link." [4] These statistics were far more convincing to staffers than a memo mandating that they follow certain precautionary steps. In Cochran's view: "Placing someone in a cyberattack drill is the safest and most effective tactic to build the company's collective security intelligence." I will go into more detail on other ways to combat social engineering ploys in the chapter on educating medical and administrative staff.

PASSWORDS, POLICIES, AND PROCEDURES

Processes, the second item on the list of broad security issues mentioned previously, brings us to the three Ps: Passwords, policies, and procedures.

Passwords fall under the category "user authentication," which is tech speak for the process of verifying that the person signing on to a computer system really *is* the person he or she claims to be. To balance strong security against user convenience, passwords need to be hard to guess but not too hard for staffers to remember (Fig. 5.1).

The password policy at Beth Israel Deaconess Medical Center (BIDMC) in Boston is worth emulating. Passwords need to be at least eight characters long and must consist of four types of characters: uppercase letters, lower case letters, numerals, and special characters like @ or #. Skeptical employees may feel this is

Objective
✓ Identify best practices to secure IT assets
and data in and out of the office

Physical Access Controls

Password Protection

▸ A strong password for your network account and other applications is a basic protection mechanism.

▸ While it is tempting to create an easy or generic password that is easy to remember, it is not very secure.

▸ Two rules for stronger passwords:

  – Create a password at least eight characters in length.

  – Password should contain at least one each:

    ▪ Capital letter

    ▪ Lowercase letter

    ▪ Number

    ▪ Special character (%,^,*,?)

Information Systems Security Awareness   20

FIGURE 5.1 Password protection advice from HHS security awareness training presentation. http://www.hhs.gov/ocio/securityprivacy/awarenesstraining/issa.pdf

overkill but they are dead wrong! There are several password cracking software programs available that allow hackers to scan millions of common passwords *per second* to locate yours. These tools typically include virtually every word in the dictionary, as well as common phrases from popular and classical literature.

Of course, asking staffers to come up with passwords that meet all the aforementioned criteria will get pushback because they are harder to remember than those that rely on a pet's name or a favorite TV character. One option is to suggest they think of a passphrase or short memorable sentence and then shorten it by using initials. So for instance, "I live at 322 Grand Avenue in Brooklyn" can become Il@322GAiB. (Notice that the password has the same upper and lower case letters that exist in the sentence, which makes it easier to remember.) It is probably best not to use one's actual street address in the passphrase, however, since intruders may have access to that information. And whatever password is used, never *ever* write it on a sticky note and paste it to a nearby workstation. That is one of the first violations HIPAA auditors will likely look for when they do a site inspection.

It is also advisable to choose a user authentication system that forces employees to follow the aforementioned guidelines on password strength; in other words, a password generation technology that rejects the creation of new passwords that are not at least eight characters long, uses a combination of lower and upper case letters, and requires at least one special character. To reduce the likelihood of unauthorized persons gaining access to your network by means of a password cracking program, it is also wise to lock out users who fail to enter the correct code after 10 attempts.

Since verifying a computer user's identity can involve more than just creating strong passwords, decision makers have to consider the use of two-factor authentication. On July 9, 2015, the federal Office of Personnel Management revealed the disturbing news that confidential information on 21.5 million people in its database had been compromised. That included the addresses, health and financial history, and other private details of more than 19 million people who had been subjected to government background checks. An additional 1.8 million people were exposed including spouses and friends [5]. Since that break-in, the government got "serious" about improving cybersecurity, but a *New York Times* analysis made it clear that such improvements would fall far short of industry standards because at present, federal computer networks are "cobbled together with out-of-date equipment and defended with the software equivalent of Bubble Wrap." [6].

One of the weaknesses in federal agencies has been user authentication. Since the aforementioned data leak, some agencies have only now begun to use a two-factor approach to verify all of their authorized users, which has been considered a basic precaution in the minds of many security specialists for years. In single factor authentication, once you enter your user name and password, you are allowed entry into the system. The two-factor approach requires a second step to harden security. It may require you to answer a few questions, for example, what was your best friend's last name or your grandmother's maiden name. Or it may require swiping an ID card or a token, or a biometric scan of your fingerprint or retina.

Getting back to our discussion about balancing security with clinician convenience and acceptance, if the second authentication procedure is too annoying, users will rebel, which is why typing in answers to one or two questions is more palatable than carrying a smart card around, and less expensive than biometric scans. However, if your organization already requires employees to wear their ID badges, adding the technology that allows it to function as the second leg in the authentication procedure is much more palatable.

HIPAA states that a healthcare organization must "verify the identity of a person requesting protected health information and the authority of any such person to have access to protected health information… if the identity or any such authority of such person is not known to the covered entity." [7]. Although that regulation does not specify two factor method, it is worth serious consideration if you want to strengthen your defenses.

ESTABLISHING EFFECTIVE GOVERNANCE

Of course, creating a set of policies and procedures to reduce the risk of a data breach or other HIPAA violation involves a lot more than mandating strong passwords. Your policies and procedures manual should cover the organization's security management process, access controls, the procedure for conducting a security risk analysis, other aspects of user authentication besides passwords, encryption protocols, how to secure workstations, how to respond to a security or privacy incident or data breach, as well as details on mobile device security, training requirements for staffers, penalties for violating security policy, responsible email usage by employees, contingency planning, and how to maintain physical security. At Beth Israel Deaconess in Boston, the security policy states that "Users must ensure that laptop computers used for BIDMC's business are secured with a laptop lock or some other equivalent physical measure when left unattended, both inside and outside of the BIDMC facilities." The medical center's policy is backed by mandatory training materials (available online through its Learning Management System), an exam, and an attestation.

To manage this long to-do list requires effective governance. The latest statistics from the American Medical Association indicate that more than 60% of physicians work in practices with 10 physicians or fewer [8]. In settings such as this, security governance takes on a very different meaning than it does in large group practices and hospitals. Nonetheless, even small practices should have someone who takes the lead in creating a preventive strategy and spells out specific tactics to help the practice comply with HIPAA regulations on privacy and security. Without real leadership and the ability of physician leaders to act as role models and champions for the rest of the staff, any policies and procedures that the practice puts in place will have a limited effect on the practice's culture. For policies and procedures to be really effective, team members have to *want* to adhere to them because they see their value and because they see practice leaders setting the example.

In larger organizations, there is the temptation to make security governance committees very technologist oriented, but if you want to win the full cooperation of your physicians, they too need to be put in decision making roles and have a prominent role in such committees. After all, they have to work with the policies and procedures that are put in place while they are "in the trenches" treating patients.

TECHNOLOGICAL SOLUTIONS

The third component in a holistic prevention strategy, technology, includes a long list of tools that may prove challenging to decision makers who did not get their degrees in computer science or work their way up the ladder learning to implement and manage these tools. The list includes firewalls, antiviral and antispyware programs, intrusion prevention systems, encryption, user authentication protocols, and audit logs. A deep understanding of these safeguards is beyond the scope of this book but my aim here is to provide enough details to allow C-suite executives and other decision makers to offer direction to those with more technical expertise. After all, you do not want to be fooled into purchasing the services of an unscrupulous security wizard who is selling you fairy dust wrapped in technobabble.

As you read through these various tools, keep in mind that there can be considerable overlap among them, with some vendors packaging more than one solution into a larger suite of services.

Encryption

Encryption is a way to disguise text or other information so that it is not recognizable to others. This means converting characters in the message into gibberish so that they cannot be read by unauthorized persons, and then having a way to decode or "decrypt" the message so that it can be read by authorized persons. To oversimplify the process, it involves turning the letters a, b, and c into x, j, and q. (Technically speaking, this process is called a substitution cypher, which is encoding, not encryption.)

Unfortunately, in today's world, simple substitution of one letter for other is far too easy for hackers to decode, so modern cryptographers use sophisticated algorithms and protect them with encryption and decryption keys that prevent others from deciphering the patient data that is supposed to remain confidential. The original patient information is referred to as plaintext and the encoded information is ciphertext (Fig. 5.2).

The algorithm converts the plaintext to ciphertext, which is based on a set of rules that tells the computer how to translate between the plaintext and the encrypted messages. For example, if we were to look at a simple substitution cipher, the rule might call for the conversion of every letter to three letters later in the alphabet, thus substituting every "a" character to a "d," "b" to an "e," and so on.

Modern cryptographic algorithms are typically based around the use of keys. The encryption key serves as the mechanism to instruct the computer how to

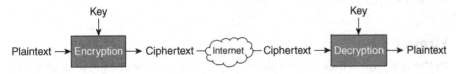

FIGURE 5.2 During the encryption process, plaintext is covered to ciphertext, which can then be transmitted across the Internet and decrypted back into plaintext.

translate the ciphertext back into a plaintext message. These keys usually come in two flavors. The first system, called symmetric encryption, requires a single key to encrypt and decrypt the message. A second approach, referred to as a public key or asymmetric cryptography, makes use of a publically available key for encryption and a separate private key for decrypting. The latter is considered more secure but is a longer process and requires more processing power.

Modern cryptographic algorithms are based around very computationally difficult mathematical problems, and the strength of the security around the encrypted message can vary with the length of the key used when it was encrypted. Choosing a strong key is one of the factors in ensuring that the message is not decrypted by unauthorized parties.

HIPAA does not mandate encryption of PHI, but if you do not encrypt the data on a mobile device and the device gets stolen or lost, you better have a pretty good reason for not encrypting the data. And in light of the fact that several healthcare organizations have been heavily fined for losing laptops containing unencrypted data, it is hard to imagine a justification that would hold up to scrutiny by the Office of Civil Rights.

Encrypting the servers within your data center poses a different set of circumstances, and some prominent health systems have chosen not to encrypt these machines because it can slow down operations; and if the data is corrupted, you are in big trouble because it then becomes irretrievable. Choosing to encrypt data in this type of setting is a judgment call. But once again, the decision not to encrypt your servers has to be justified because the patient data still has to conform to the HIPAA security rule requiring it to be protected, so other security measures should be in place.

If your organization uses a wireless network, it is important to encrypt this pathway as well. Wi-Fi networks can be dangerously insecure, which means anyone who logs onto the Internet at a public café is at risk. WPA2 is a first step toward securing these transmissions. Referred to as Wi-Fi Protected Access Version 2, this approach helps protect data as it is transmitted by creating a unique encryption key for each device connected to the network. WPA2 relies on a well-respected security standard called Advanced Encryption Standard or AES and can be FIPS 140-2 compliant if implemented properly [9]. (FIPS compliant means it is consistent with the Federal Information Processing Standards for non-military government agencies.)

Firewalls

In the real world, that is, the one not composed of 0s and 1s, a firewall separates your car's engine compartment from the cabin, physically protecting it in case the engine bursts into flames. In cyberspace, firewalls have a similar function; they are either hardware or software that serves as the first line of defense, offering a measure of protection by blocking suspicious traffic from the Internet. They can also be placed within your organization's network to shield off sensitive information from unauthorized internal users.

On a personal computer, a firewall is typically built into a Netgear or Linksys router that sends data to your home network. Assuming your computer also has an antimalware program by Norton, MacAfee, or another vendor, there is likely software in that program that serves as a firewall as well. But if you are running a medical practice, hospital, or other organization that handles PHI, you want to take things to the next level, and that requires a deeper understanding of the types of firewalls available and where they are best positioned. Using the services of a good consultant also makes sense to help manage said firewalls.

Three common types of firewalls are packet filters, stateful inspection firewalls, and application gateways. To make sense of a packet filter, it helps to be familiar with two terms used in the IT community: packets and IP addresses. A packet is a chunk of data that includes a portion of the actual information you want to send or receive—for example, a pdf containing a patient's record—referred to as the "payload". The packet also contains addressing information, including the sender's and recipient's addresses. If the size of the payload file is too large, it is split among the payloads of a great number of packets due to its size. The addressing information is referred to as an IP address, which is the unique set of digits that identifies what computer is sending the data; a separate IP address exists to identify the computer that receives it. Computers that communicate over the internet are usually assigned a unique string of numbers. The internet service provider will typically assign a number, which can look something like this: 10.239.115.148. If your packet firewall does not like a particular source IP address, it will prevent the entire data packet from passing through and infecting your network.

If you can visualize a simplified flow chart describing your organization's connection to the internet, start with point A, your internet service provider (ISP), and follow the arrow pointing from the ISP to your outer boundary router, which contains a packet filter, and then an arrow from the router to a second stronger firewall that performs stateful inspection. A third tool, the application gateway, will likely be placed somewhere in the pathway as well so that all three firewalls need to be passed through before anyone—including hackers— can reach the sensitive data at the heart of your network.

One common approach to firewall management is to have the packet filter take a "guilty until proven innocent" position—known in firewall terminology as default deny—in which it blocks all traffic by default. Then someone on the security team or network team adds rules that include exceptions to this default to allow selected information to pass through. Glen Clarke gives a simple example of how this might work in the CompTIA Security+ certification guide:

"If you have a web server that you want to expose to the Internet, you would block all traffic except TCP port 80 on which web server traffic runs." [10]. (However, at least ports 80 and 443 would need to be available for a web server to function properly.)

A packet filtering firewall derives its name from its ability to block or allow packets of data on the basis of source and/or destination IP addresses, ports, and protocols contained within the packets. For example, your clinicians would probably consider the *New England Journal of Medicine* web site useful and trustworthy, so a packet of information with the source IP address of the NEJM web site could be allowed to pass through the filter to reach your private network. But assume for the moment that you decide that any information from youtube.com or facebook.com is too dangerous to allow into your private network. In that case, your packet filter could deny access from their IP addresses.

Unfortunately packet filters still miss a lot of malicious content, so the data will typically pass through a stateful inspection filter in the same device. To understand how this firewall works, it helps to understand the concept of a "three-way handshake" that is used to establish a legitimate connection between the internet and a computer network. It is a series of three messages sent back and forth between the sending computer and the receiving computer that establishes a correct connection. If a hacker were to try to send a packet of malicious information to your organization but did not perform this 3-way handshake procedure, the stateful filter would block the data transfer. They are called stateful firewalls because they track the state of the communication process to determine if the path of the information is following standard protocols.

Finally, a word about the third type of firewall: Whether you are logging onto a weather app, Google docs, or an online dose calculator, these applications can all be infected with malicious computer code that can find its way onto your network as clinicians and administrators tap into these conveniences. Application gateways or filters can block malicious commands embedded in these sources. Although packet firewalls will stop an invasion by blocking an IP address associated with some malicious code, and a stateful filter will block the infection if the sender has not followed the usual communication pathways, an application gateway can actually look inside the malicious code—the payload within the packet—to identify harmful commands.

Decision makers working in the healthcare community may wonder: Does HIPAA require the installment of firewalls? Although there is no direct mandate, or even an addressable standard in HIPAA that calls for firewalls, it is worth mentioning that healthcare organizations that have reported data breaches have been fined because their firewalls were not working. Idaho State

University (ISU), for instance, was fined $400,000 because they allowed un-authorized access to ePHI. The Office of Civil Rights report on the incident stated: "The HHS Office for Civil Rights (OCR) opened an investigation after ISU notified HHS of the breach in which the ePHI of approximately 17,500 patients was unsecured for at least 10 months, due to the disabling of firewall protections at servers maintained by ISU…. OCR concluded that ISU did not apply proper security measures and policies to address risks to ePHI and did not have procedures for routine review of their information system in place, which could have detected the firewall breach much sooner." [11].

Choosing the types of firewalls to install in your facility is an individualized decision but as a general rule, it is best to get the strongest products you can afford. One reliable option for smaller medical practices is Cisco's small business RV series routers.

Antimalware/Antiviral Software

Before you can make an intelligent decision about the type of antimalware program to invest in, it helps to understand what the term malware currently encompasses. In the broadest sense, malware is any type of software with mali-cious intent. That intent can include not just the thief of confidential patient information but the disruption of your computer system's functioning, de-struction of data, or even locking up your system's data so that it cannot be ac-cessed by authorized users until you pay a ransom for its release. In addition to viruses, your software should be able to detect Trojans, bots, worms, spyware, and rootkits. I will briefly discuss some of these infectious agents.

A digital virus, similar to its biological counterpart, has the ability to copy itself once inside a computer and hide until an opportune moment. Eventually the computer user takes some action that triggers the malware to do its mischief. Once the time bomb goes off, the malware delivers its "payload" and the user has to deal with the consequences. Those consequences may simply be an ob-scene sentence flashing across the screen, or slowing down the machine's pro-cessing ability, or stealing passwords.

A Trojan derives its name from the fact that it can look like a normal file that has some value to the user, which tricks users into downloading it. The infec-tion can result in stolen data, modification of files, or keylogging, which en-ables outsiders to record every keystroke you enter into your computer.

Similarly some spyware has the ability to track a user's activities and identify each keystroke as you type, which means it may be able to read your social se-curity number, date of birth, and password as you type them on the keyboard.

What makes worms so hideous is that they do not need a human computer user to trigger them, unlike a traditional virus. A worm might send out hundreds of copies of itself by attacking a user's email list and sending a copy to all your contacts.

When looking for an antimalware program, choose one that detects not just your garden variety viruses but other types of malware. Also make sure the software is installed on all your machines. So email servers should have email server antimalware software, workstations should have desktop protection, and servers should have protective programs designed for their protection.

Equally important, these programs need to be set up to automatically download regular updates. New malware shows up every day so without updates the program is almost useless. What that also means is if for some reason you disconnect from the internet for an extended period of time, your software will no longer be up to date since the program cannot contact the antimalware company to look for the updates. Once a new antimalware program is installed, you will want to instruct the software to setup a schedule to regularly scan each machine.

While we are on the subject of updates, someone in your office or department should be responsible for checking for updates to all your applications and your operating system. If Windows, for instance, comes out with an update, it is often because the company has detected some security hole in its previous version, which the new patch plugs up. One option is to set up the computer for automatic Windows updates.

One of the main disadvantages of antimalware programs, unfortunately, is that it is not possible to write a set of signatures to cover all known malware at all times. There is always a lag between the time the virus goes live and the time the antimalware vendor is able to create an antidote and distribute it to its customers. That interval is when you are most vulnerable, and the time your system needs to rely on other defenses.

Antimalware vendors are now moving beyond traditional programs that rely on the signature-based approach that only looks for the digital fingerprints of malware after they have been discovered. Symantec Endpoint Protection, for instance, is one of several programs that go beyond the basics, using more sophisticated analytics and reputation-based security. [12] Reputation-based security analyzes billions of files floating around the world and labels them as having either a good or bad reputation. Once assigned, the antimalware program can block the suspicious ones.

One of the biggest security threats to individual computers and networks are web sites that contain malicious content, which can be automatically loaded onto your system once you open the web site in a browser. Companies such as McAfee, Norton, and others offer antimalware suites that now contain much more than standard signature-based programs. They can also help detect fraudulent and infected web sites. Norton's Internet Security suite can also help detect infected web sites during an internet search, rating the level of risk for each of the search results, allowing you to decide what to do before you click on the link.

Access Control

We discussed some basic access controls earlier in the chapter, including passwords and two-factor authentication, but there is more that can be done in this area. HIPAA discusses this part of the security equation in standard 164.308 and 164.312. Regulation 164.312(a)(1) states in part: "Implement technical policies and procedures for electronic information systems that maintain electronic protected health information to allow access only to those persons or software programs that have been granted access rights ...."

Access control requires a three-pronged approach, addressing physical, administrative, and technological safeguards.

Your organization needs adequate physical barriers to prevent unauthorized persons from gaining access to your computer network, to individual desktops, and to mobile devices, including obvious things such as locked doors, employee badges, and so on. It also requires administrative measures, including a policy and procedures manual that spells out who is entitled to view what type of information.

Physicians should be granted access to PHI for their patients while certain administrative staffers may not require the same level of access. Similarly, analysts, outside IT consultants, accountants, and other internal and external users may each require different types of access. Collectively this is referred to as *role-based* access control. Once a set of roles have been established, your IT team or consultant can implement the technical solutions needed to enforce the policy. Tom Walsh provides a sample role-based access control matrix in a recent HIMSS publication [13].

Intrusion Detection and Intrusion Prevention Systems

If you are a decision maker without an in-depth background in information technology, Webopedia is a good source to make sense of things. It has a simple way of describing IDS: "Used in computer security, intrusion detection refers to the process of monitoring computer and network activities and analyzing those events to look for signs of intrusion in your system." [14]. These tools, which may be hardware boxes and software, can monitor traffic on an individual computer—sometimes referred to as a client or host computer—and a network of computers linked together. Once the tool detects suspicious activity, it will log it and alert an IT administrator. Intrusion prevention systems, on the other hand, will take action to block the threat before it happens.

Depending on the type of system you purchase, it may accomplish these tasks using a signature-based database or an anomaly-based approach. A signature-based system, like a signature-based antimalware program, contains the digital fingerprints of commonly used hacker tactics, a port scan for example. It may spot attack signatures that are used by a worm or virus. An anomaly-based system sets up a baseline of normal computer or network activities and then looks for anything outside these norms, labelling it as abnormal and suspicious.

Typically an IDS consists of sensors, an analysis engine, and a console or dashboard that allows an IT administrator to receive alerts about suspicious activity and to set up the functioning of the tool.

Faxing Solutions

HIPAA's Privacy Rule states that physicians can use fax services to send a copy of a patient's records to another healthcare provider but specifies that "covered health care providers apply reasonable safeguards when making these communications to protect the information from inappropriate use or disclosure. These safeguards may vary depending on the mode of communication used. For example, when faxing protected health information to a telephone number that is not regularly used, a reasonable safeguard may involve a provider first confirming the fax number with the intended recipient. Similarly, a covered entity may pre-program frequently used numbers directly into the fax machine to avoid misdirecting the information."

These guidelines seem pretty straightforward, but think back to the number of times you have seen important documents sitting unattended at a fax machine and you begin to see the potential for HIPAA violations. If an OCR auditor happens to walk by and sees a lab report with a patient's name on it, it could spell trouble. Many healthcare providers have opted for an internet-based fax service to bypass such security issues. With this type of service, you either send a fax as an unsecured email attachment—not the best option if you want to stay HIPAA compliant—or use a secure server that sends an email notice to tell the recipient that a fax is available, at which point he or she logs on to a secure, encryption-protected inbox to pick up the fax. OpenText and eFax are two vendors that offer security features to help providers comply with government regulations.

Auditing Your Computer Systems

In the context of information security, the term auditing can mean many different things. It can refer to federal officials coming in to audit your compliance with HIPAA or Meaningful Use. Or it can refer to the mock audits performed by private consultants to help the organization become compliant with regulations. But you may also hear security specialists refer to "audit controls," which have a different connotation.

Electronic records can generate activity logs—assuming that the application housing them is properly configured to do so—and email systems can spit out lists of users. Firewalls, antimalware programs, servers, and workstations can also provide logs that can be reviewed to look for suspicious activity, unauthorized access, and other types of intelligence to help an organization prevent a data breach or detect it early on. Analyzing these logs can also help you determine if someone on staff who is authorized to use the system is looking at PHI outside the scope of his job description, or reveal the fact that two or more users are sharing the same password.

HIPAA requires audit controls, as stated in standard 164.308(a)(1)(ii)(D): "Implement hardware, software, and/or procedural mechanisms that record and examine activity in information systems that contain or use electronic protected health information." The Centers for Medicare and Medicaid Services does not spell out exactly what you should be auditing or how you should audit it, but expects you to use your risk analysis and to take into account your technological capabilities to determine a reasonable and appropriate approach.

One of the biggest problems in complying with this HIPAA standard is that computers generate *enormous* amounts of auditable data, and many healthcare providers have a difficult time managing it or finding the time to analyze it. A good place to start is with the *Guide to Computer Security Log Management*, published by the National Institute of Standards and Technology. You should also become familiar with a healthcare IT organization called the American Health Information Management Association (AHIMA). They offer several valuable resources, including a primer entitled "Security Audits of Electronic Health Information." [15] There are also commercially available audit trail management tools to help deal with the data avalanche.

Making Email More Secure

In 2015, news outlets reported that Hillary Clinton had used her personal email account to send or receive classified information—rather than take advantage of the more secure email system provided by the US State department. Although a healthcare organization may not need to protect state secrets, it still needs to take steps to harden email transmissions.

The HIPAA Security Rule says you must "Implement technical security measures to guard against unauthorized access to electronic protected health information that is being transmitted over an electronic communications network." This standard is spelled out at 45 CFR 164.312(e)(1). As with many HIPAA standards, the law also lists what it refers to as "implementation specifications," which are ways to put the standard into everyday practice. For this standard, there are two specifications: Integrity controls and encryption, both of which are addressable [16].

Maintaining the integrity of PHI as it has been transmitted means preventing it from being altered or "improperly modified" according to HIPAA. Encryption was discussed earlier in the chapter and since it is an addressable specification, it is not mandated. HIPAA regulations express the issue this way: "Implement a mechanism to encrypt electronic protected health information whenever deemed appropriate." Most security specialists recognize the fact that the only effective way to protect PHI sent through an email is by means of encryption.

There are two separate but related issues here, namely how to communicate by email with other healthcare organizations or clinicians, and how to communicate with patients. The latter is addressed directly in a Q and A from the Office for Civil Rights. In answer to the question: "Does the HIPAA Privacy Rule permit health care providers to use e-mail to discuss health issues and treatment with their patients?" OCR states: "[W]hile the Privacy Rule does not prohibit the use of unencrypted e-mail for treatment-related communications between health care providers and patients, other safeguards should be applied to reasonably protect privacy, such as limiting the amount or type of information disclosed through the unencrypted e-mail." The same OCR answer goes on to caution, however: "If the provider feels the patient may not be aware of the possible risks of using unencrypted e-mail, or has concerns about potential liability, the provider can alert the patient of those risks, and let the patient decide whether to continue e-mail communications." With that caveat in mind, it is best to inform all patients that there are risks involved in standard email communication and receive their permission to use it [17].

Email communication between healthcare organizations gets more complicated. It is worth noting that when OCR was asked about the HIPAA Privacy Rule that permits healthcare providers to share PHI with other healthcare organizations, it stated that "A physician may consult with another physician by e-mail about a patient's condition." But there are no comments about the acceptability of unencrypted email in the OCR response, only that the provider needs to apply reasonable safeguards. With that in mind, one can read between the lines here and come to the conclusion that encrypted email is the best way to stay off the OCR "wall of shame", the list of healthcare organizations and business associates that have had data breaches affecting 500 or more patients.

A quick search of that OCR database lists several violations that involved email. Here is a sampling of what took place:

- *Hospice of the Chesapeake*: an employee emailed spreadsheets containing ePHI of more than 7000 patients to a personal email account and a third party may have viewed the data, which contained names, addresses, conditions, and diagnoses.
- *Geisinger Wyoming Valley Medical Center*: A staff physician emailed PHI of about 2900 patients to his home email account while working on an analysis. OCR stated: "Following the breach, the CE sanctioned the physician and implemented a plan to auto-encrypt all PHI sent through email. As a result of OCR's investigation, the CE improved its physical safeguards and retrained employees."
- *Georgetown University Hospital*: A hospital employee emailed PHI to an offsite research office, which was not part of the hospital. The research office stored the information on an external hard drive that was later stolen [18].

Several companies offer email encryption software including Cisco, McAfee, Symantec, Trend Micro, ProofPoint, Microsoft, and Google.

As mentioned earlier, phishing scams are a major headache in healthcare these days and they are typically encountered through an organization's email system. The chapter on staff education will go into more detail on how to sidestep these traps.

ESTABLISHING PHYSICAL SAFEGUARDS

Some IT professionals find the topic boring because it is not very technological; but as a decision maker it is just as critical as firewalls, encryption, and anti-malware software. Regardless of the size of your organization, the Department of Health and Human Services expects you to make a reasonable effort to keep unauthorized users away from PHI through the use of locked doors and a host of other common sense measures.

Federal regulation 45 C.F.R. 164.310(a) states that: "A covered entity must limit physical access to its facilities while ensuring that authorized access is allowed." 45 C.F.R.164.310(b) and (c) say a "covered entity must implement policies and procedures to specify proper use of and access to workstations and electronic media." HIPAA also stipulates that "A covered entity also must have in place policies and procedures regarding the transfer, removal, disposal, and re-use of electronic media, to ensure appropriate protection of electronic protected health information (e-PHI)" at 45 C.F.R. 164.310(d).

How does this all translate in the real world? If your hardware is located in your facility, it means placing servers and other critical infrastructure in a locked, temperature controlled room. The purpose of the lock may be obvious, but the purpose of the temperature control—from a HIPAA compliance perspective—may not be. If your hardware fails because it gets too hot in the computer room, not only does it become difficult to perform day to day operations, it also deprives patients of access to their medical information, which is mandated by federal regulations.

Other physical protections can include biometrics or magnetic-strip ID badges. It should also include an emergency response plan to retrieve data in the event of a fire, storm, or earthquake. HIPAA also requires you to physically safeguard any laptops, CDs, external hard drives, thumb drives, and other media containing patient information to prevent theft and destruction.

Similarly, whenever you have to discard PHI, it needs to be done safely. More than one healthcare organization has been fined for dumping paper files containing sensitive information in open trash bins outside their facility, or selling or donating old computers, fax machines, and photocopiers that contain patient data. Shedders to destroy paper files, CDs, and the like are a good idea.

If on the other hand, your PHI resides in the cloud, resting on a vendor's servers, you should have reassurances that the vendor has physical safeguards in place.

PROTECTING BIG DATA

This is one of the more challenging issues for healthcare decision makers to manage. The term itself is poorly defined, meaning different things to different people. But for simplicity's sake, big data has three main attributes—often referred to as the three Vs. It consists of a huge *volume* of data, typically in the petabyte range. One petabyte is equivalent to 1024 terabytes (Tb). Many personal computers now come with a hard drive containing a single terabyte, which is about 1000 gigabytes. To put these numbers into perspective, a small-to-medium size medical practice may contain about 2 terabytes of data in its computers. The Library of Congress houses more than 200 Tb of data. A large academic medical center and affiliated medical school can have 3–4 petabytes of clinical and research data in its systems.

The second V is *velocity*, which refers to the high-powered, high-speed digital tools needed to quickly analyze the massive amounts of data. The third V is *variety*. Depending on the nature of your organization and its goals, that can include input from wearable medical devices, wireless monitors, hours of video and other radiological images, marketing data gleaned from patient satisfaction surveys, Twitter feeds, and so on.

In many ways, protecting these massive amounts of data is similar to protecting data in EHRs, practice management programs, and other more traditional sources. But in some ways it is different. Security measures in healthcare organizations have traditionally been focused on "perimeter defense," in other words, building a protective wall around an internal network through the use of firewalls, antimalware programs, and locked server rooms to keep outsiders outside. Healthcare organizations that are doing big data analytics need these safeguards, but they are not enough because these setups may not *have* a perimeter—at least not in the usual sense. Adam Boone, with Certes, a company that provides security for data networks, points out that "The perimeter, firewall-based infrastructure was designed to keep data inside and the bad guys outside. Now data flows everywhere, so a perimeter-based model makes a lot less sense. The perimeter is crumbling and the idea of a secure, trusted network environment is increasingly old fashioned."

Put another way, big data is about "distributed computing." The internet itself is a form of distributed computing, with routers, network access points, repeaters, hubs, and gateways around the world all tied together. Traditional security protections that can wall off a small medical practice's PHI would do nothing to protect PHI if it were available on the Internet; nor can it adequately protect a healthcare provider that is tapping into online applications, external data sources, the cloud, mobile devices, transaction logs, Hadoop, and enterprise data warehouse from various locations.

One option that can reduce the risk of compromising PHI that resides in a database is de-identification or anonymization, which removes all data elements that would allow an unauthorized user to figure out who the patients are. The Department of Health and Human Services provides several resources to help healthcare organizations strip sensitive information from their files and adhere to the HIPAA Privacy Rule [19].

Stripping identifying details from patient records would be valuable in a database that is being used to conduct clinical research, in which you may only need to know how many patients suffered from osteoarthritis and whether or not they used a certain medication, for example, but do not need their names or other personal identifying features.

HHS outlines two acceptable ways to de-identify PHI: expert determination and safe harbor. For the former, you need to have an expert to determine that the method used to strip out sensitive details resulted in a very small risk that someone would be able to figure out who the patients were based on the information that remained in the database. The expert works with the organization to determine appropriate statistical and scientific methods to mitigate the risk of identification and then documents the methods used.

The safe harbor approach, described in HIPAA regulation 164.514(b), requires removal of a long list of identifiers, including not just the patient's name but his or her street address, birth date, hospital admission date, telephone numbers, email addresses, social security numbers, to name a few.

If you are working with large data sets stretched out across the globe, you may also want to strengthen the user authentication procedure. Earlier in the chapter, we discussed strong passwords, two-factor authentication, and the need to balance security with ease of use so as not to turn off busy clinicians. In big-data analytics, the need to keep things quick and easy for clinicians on the front lines is not usually an issue so a more sophisticated authentication procedure like Kerberos authentication can be used to add another layer of security in this setting. The approach requires encrypted passwords, secret keys, and a six step back and forth process between the user's workstation, the Kerberos Key Distribution Center, and the server containing the database you are trying to access [20].

We have only scratched the surface on this topic. Big data initiatives can generate real insights that improve patient care, push forward new business decisions, and much more, but diving into this relatively new arena is not for the inexperienced. One recent survey found that about three out of four senior level IT and security specialists were worried about the inability to secure data in this kind of setting. In light of such concerns, you will want to hire IT specialists and security experts who thoroughly know this specialized field. Also consider reaching out to vendors such as Cloudera, Hortonworks, and IBM for solutions to plug the security gaps [21].

TESTING YOUR NETWORK SECURITY

If you decide to invest significant capital and manpower to strengthen your organization's security, you will want to know that the investment is paying dividends. One way to do that is to evaluate its strength, a process called penetration testing, which involves hiring someone to put on the "black hat" and try to break into the organization's computer system as an unauthorized user to see how easy it is to gain access to PHI.

The relevant HIPAA standard, 164.308(a)(8), states that you need to "Perform a periodic technical and nontechnical evaluation, based initially upon the standards implemented under this [Security] rule and subsequently, in response to environmental or operational changes affecting the security of electronic protected health information..." As you may recall from earlier in the chapter, some HIPAA standards are accompanied by implementation specifications that dictate how the standard should be carried out. This standard has no such specifications. But it is worth noting that the National

Institute of Standards and Technology (NIST), in its guide to implementing HIPAA's Security Rule, recommends penetration testing to fulfill this particular standard if it "has been determined to be reasonable and appropriate."[22]

Frankly, having a penetration test done makes business sense. Any would-be hacker can now go online and purchase a do-it-yourself kit—called script kiddies—that can help break into a computer network, and bookstores sell how-to manuals on hacking as well. In recent years, the hacker community has also come to include organized crime groups and nation states. With this kind of brain power knocking at your door, healthcare organizations need to look at their network through the eyes of a hacker to detect their vulnerabilities before the cybercriminals do.

CompTIA, a nonprofit trade association that certifies computer technicians and other IT professionals, explains that "a penetration test is one of the best ways to verify that a threat actually exists because you are performing the exact types of action a hacker would perform to exploit the system." [23]. The test can take many different forms. The tester might do what Tom Cochran of Atlanta Media did to prove to his staff that they were susceptible to a phishing attack by sending out a fake email scam. Or it can attempt to crack your computer system's firewall, or use a password cracking program to break into an employee's user account, and use manual or automated techniques to try to penetrate your servers, web applications, wireless network, mobile devices and much more. Some testers will also test your organization's physical barriers by posing as a repairman, for instance, to see if he can get past the front desk and gain access to a senior manager's office.

There are a variety of scenarios, but whichever you decide on, make sure a written agreement between your organization and the pen tester spells out the responsibilities of each party in detail. And be aware that some types of tests can cause a computer system to crash, which means you can temporarily lose access to data used in day to day operations. After all, these white knight hackers are trying to disrupt things.

Perhaps it goes without saying, but in choosing a pen tester, you want to find someone with good references; hiring a bad guy posing as a good guy can wreak havoc. ZDNet has posted a set of tips to help decision makers choose wisely [24].

If you consider penetration testing too extreme for your organization, another option is vulnerability testing, also called a vulnerability assessment. Vulnerability testing looks for weaknesses in your computer but does not attempt to exploit them. Testers have a variety software tools available to help scan a network for weaknesses.

CYBERSECURITY INSURANCE

Insurance is a double-edged sword. It can save businesses millions of dollars by protecting them against credible threats, but it can also waste money defending against extremely remote dangers that are very unlikely to materialize. It can also give a manager a false sense of security.

Of course, in today's environment, a data breach is not a remote possibility, which is why some security specialists recommend cybersecurity insurance. Others are less enthusiastic and emphasize that insurance is no substitute for robust security measures.

Mac McMillian, CEO of CynergisTek, a security services company, also emphasizes the limitations of these policies. "Insurers limit their liability and their exposure by limiting what they cover or making the underwriting provisions very specific…. I hear of a lot of healthcare providers who are getting $10 million of coverage but some breaches have cost providers hundreds of millions of dollars… I still believe having cyber insurance is a good idea as long as you understand its limitations. If you have a major breach that ends up with a class action lawsuit and all the other typical costs, nine times out of ten, cybersecurity insurance is not going to cover it all."

References

[1] S. Morse. Safeguarding against cyberattacks, Healthcare Finance, 2015, p. 44.

[2] T. Walsh, Risk management and strategic planning, in: T.W. Herzig (Ed.), Information Security in Healthcare, Healthcare Information and Management Systems Society, Chicago, 2010, pp. 18.

[3] A. Savvas. 91% of cyberattacks begin with spear phishing email, TechWorld. http://www.techworld.com/news/security/91-of-cyberattacks-begin-with-spear-phishing-email-3413574/, 2012.

[4] T. Cochran. Why I phished my own company, Harvard Business Review. https://hbr.org/2013/06/why-i-phished-my-own-company/, 2013.

[5] H.J. Davis. Hacking of government computers exposed 21.5 million people, New York Times, http://www.nytimes.com/2015/07/10/us/office-of-personnel-management-hackers-got-data-of-millions.html?_r=0, 2015.

[6] M. Shear, N. Perlroth. Us vs hackers; still lopsided, New York Times, p A1. http://www.nytimes.com/2015/07/19/us/us-vs-hackers-still-lopsided-despite-years-of-warnings-and-a-recent-push.html, 2015.

[7] Cornell University Law School. 45 CFR 164.514 - Other requirements relating to uses and disclosures of protected health information. https://www.law.cornell.edu/cfr/text/45/164.514.

[8] J. Commins. Most physicians work in small practices, MedpageToday. http://www.medpagetoday.com/PrimaryCare/GeneralPrimaryCare/52539, 2015.

[9] T.W. Herzig, T. Walsh, L.A. Gallagher. Implementing Information Security in Healthcare: Building A Security Program, Chicago, Healthcare Information and Management Systems Society, 2013, p. 114.

[10] G.E. Clarke, CompTIA Security+ Certification Study Guide, second ed., New York: McGraw Hill, (2014) p. 333.

[11] HHS.gov. Idaho State University settles HIPAA security case for $400,000. http://www.hhs.gov/ocr/privacy/hipaa/enforcement/examples/isu-agreement-press-release.html.html, 2013.

[12] Symantec Security Series: Symantec Insight. https://www.youtube.com/watch?v=HxbPScdt-3s.

[13] B. Evans, Access control program, in: T.W. Herzig, T. Walsh, L.S. Gallagher (Eds.), Implementing Information Security in Healthcare: Building a Security, Chicago: HIMSS, 2013, p. 86.

[14] Beal V. Intrusion detection (IDS) and prevention (IPS) systems. http://www.webopedia.com/DidYouKnow/Computer_Science/intrusion_detection_prevention.asp, 2015.

[15] AHIMA. Security audits of electronic health information (updated). http://library.ahima.org/xpedio/groups/public/documents/ahima/bok1_048702.hcsp?dDocName=bok1_048702, 2011.

[16] Cornell University Law School. 45 CFR 164.312 - Technical safeguards. https://www.law.cornell.edu/cfr/text/45/164.312.

[17] Department of Health and Human Services Office for Civil Rights. Does the HIPAA Privacy Rule permit health care providers to use e-mail to discuss health issues and treatment with their patients? http://www.hhs.gov/ocr/privacy/hipaa/faq/health_information_technology/570.html, 2008.

[18] US Department of Health and Human Services Office for Civil Rights. Breaches affecting 500 or more individuals. https://ocrportal.hhs.gov/ocr/breach/breach_report.jsf.

[19] US Department of Health and Human Services Office for Civil Rights. Guidance regarding methods for de-identification of protected health information in accordance with the Health Insurance Portability and Accountability Act (HIPAA) Privacy Rule. http://www.hhs.gov/ocr/privacy/hipaa/understanding/coveredentities/De-identification/guidance.html.

[20] Intel AMT implementation and reference guide. Introduction to Kerberos authentication. https://software.intel.com/sites/manageability/AMT_Implementation_and_Reference_Guide/default.htm?turl=WordDocuments%2Fintroductiontokerberosauthentication.htm.

[21] S. Pramanick. Addressing big data security. IBM Big Data and Analytics Hub. http://www.ibmbigdatahub.com/blog/addressing-big-data-security, 2013.

[22] National Institute of Standards and Technology. An introductory resource guide for implementing the Health Insurance Portability and Accountability Act (HIPAA) Security Rule. http://www.hhs.gov/ocr/privacy/hipaa/administrative/securityrule/nist80066.pdf, 2008.

[23] G.E. Clarke, CompTIA Security+Certification Study Guide, New York: McGraw Hill, (2014).

[24] V. Blue. 10 things you need to know before hiring penetration testers, ZDNet. http://www.zdnet.com/article/10-things-you-need-to-know-before-hiring-penetration-testers/, 2014.

CHAPTER 6

Mobile Device Security

Surveys suggest that nearly nine out of ten physicians use smartphones or tablets in the workplace, which only emphasizes the need for proper security on these devices [1].

As a decision maker, you need to weigh several issues as you determine what type of mobile device policy should be put in place, and what type of security technology to invest in. Among the decisions to make: Should you even allow mobile devices to have access to your computer system; if you do allow them access, should they only be devices vetted and purchased by the organization; or will you allow clinicians and other staff members to use their own device to gain access to patient data—the so-called BYOD or Bring Your Own Device movement.

Regardless of which direction you go in, there are several basic safeguards to put in place to reduce the risk of a HIPAA violation or data breach.

THINKING STRATEGICALLY

Before putting these safeguards in place, you need a management strategy. The Department of Health and Human Services suggests a 5 step plan: decide; assess; identify; develop, document, and implement; and train.

Step one, *deciding* whether to even allow mobile devices to receive, transmit or store PHI, needs to be thought through carefully in light of all the risks associated with that move. Among them: they are much easier to steal than a desktop computer, and they are often lost—not usually a problem with a desktop computer. There is also the risk of malware infection, especially if the device is used on an unsecured Wi-Fi network. And using an unsecured wireless network is a hard temptation to resist for physicians and business executives who spend a lot of time in airports, hotel rooms, or at Wi-Fi-equipped cafés.

If a staffer's family member gets their hands on the device to surf the web or download the latest music videos, the risk of downloading a virus increases exponentially. And there is also the possibility that the family member will see PHI that they are forbidden by law to view. Suppose for the sake of this discussion, your hospital just admitted a movie celebrity for observation. That would pose a big temptation to a teenage member of the household to want to snoop into their medical records, which may be accessible on one of your physician's tablets.

Assess, step 2, is much like the risk-assessment process described in an earlier chapter. The analysis must weigh all the pros and cons and look for existing security gaps in your current network that can be exploited by someone who gains access through a stolen or lost mobile device.

You will also need to *identify* your organization's mobile risk management strategy and put in place safeguards to mitigate the likelihood of a HIPAA violation or data breach. I will discuss specific safeguards subsequently.

As you *develop and document* your mobile device management plan, you will need to answer several questions:

- Have you taken inventory? You cannot manage a collection of phones, laptops, and tablets unless you start with a complete list of all the devices that have access to your network.
- Is someone assigned the responsibility of managing these devices, making sure they comply with your policies and procedures manual?
- Have you spelled out a BYOD policy, if you decide to allow personal devices on the network?
- Will you allow employees to gain access to the organization's network while at home or traveling?
- Do you have a policy for deactivating mobile devices if an employee leaves the organization?
- Will you allow PHI to be stored on the mobile device?
- What kind of *training* will you provide employees who use a mobile device for work purposes?

COVERING THE BASICS

Many of the physical, administrative, and technological safeguards required to protect your computer network also apply to mobile devices, with some variations.

Physical safeguards may seem obvious but are often overlooked by clinicians and administrative staff because they can be inconvenient to implement. They include storing a smartphone, laptop, or tablet in a locked desk drawer, keeping the device within sight at all times, not allowing others to use the device, and putting wire locks on laptops and tablets to secure them to a desk.

In chapter 5: Reducing the Risk of a Data Breach, encryption basics have been discussed. The need for encryption on smartphones, tablets, and laptops is especially important if your organization allows employees to store PHI on the device. Several providers have had to pay heavy HIPPA-related fines because someone in the organization lost an unencrypted mobile device containing sensitive data. The federal Office of Civil Rights (OCR) offers guidelines on how to render PHI unusable, unreadable, and indecipherable to unauthorized users, stating that you have two HIPAA compliant options: Either destroy the media on which the PHI is stored or recorded, or encrypt it.

Obviously there is a lot of patient data that cannot be destroyed, so when that is the case, it should be encrypted "at rest" and "in motion." In other words, the encryption software needs to protect PHI stored in the device itself (or on the external media, for example, a thumb drive or DVD). And the PHI needs to be protected as it is moved from place to place, typically by means of email or text messaging, network transfers, backup tapes, thumb drives and so on. Valid encryption processes for at rest and in motion PHI are spelled out in more detail on the OCR site [2].

DataMotion and Trend Micro, like many comparable vendors, offer a secure mail service; their purpose is to encrypt messages when they leave a smartphone, and through their entire journey across the internet until they arrive in a recipient's inbox. DataMotion uses a thoughtful analogy to explain the risk of sending unsecured email, even when the computer from which you send the message is secure and the recipient's computer is secured. It is like writing a private message on a post card and putting it in the mail box. Yes, you can trust the US Post Office to deliver it, but few of us are naïve enough to believe no one will read it before it reaches its destination. Both vendors offer an encrypted email service for a healthcare provider's in-house servers, and as a cloud service.

Another option is a virtual private network or VPN, which also encrypts data as it is sent across a Wi-Fi connection, for example. Using a secure browser connection has some advantages as well. In the address section at the top of your browser, you will see an "s" after the "http" to verify that it is relatively secure. HHS also recommends turning off Wi-Fi capability, Bluetooth, and location services in the mobile device's settings section when they are not needed. With these services turned on, it may be possible for unauthorized users to gain access to PHI even when you are *not* trying to connect to a network [3].

Strong passwords are just as important on mobile devices as they are on workstations—perhaps more so. As I mentioned in the last chapter, the best passwords include at least one upper case and one lower case letter, a number, and a special character like ^ or *. Some providers, including Partners Healthcare in Massachusetts, also send employees reminders on their mobile device to change their password regularly. The device should also be set up to automatically lock after a short period of time so unauthorized persons have a more difficult time accessing the data if it is lost or stolen.

Similarly, installing an antimalware program on each mobile device that has access to PHI makes sense; many cautious physicians who would not think of using a desktop computer without installing antimalware software do not think twice about using a tablet or smartphone that is completely "naked." (See Box A for more on mobile antimalware programs). You should also add firewalls to mobile devices, a topic that was also discussed in the last chapter.

Another risk is loading an untrustworthy mobile app onto your device, that is, one that is infected or that will copy your address book or other private information and send it to someone else. In 2012, for example, Google removed several mobile apps from its Android store for Angry Birds, a popular game program, because they contained spyware. And the security firm Sophos discovered a mobile version of Angry birds that contained a Trojan, a rather vicious piece of malware that can allow hackers access to sensitive data [4]. (See Box B on page 79 for more on the risk of loading mobile apps onto a phone.)

BOX A INSTALLING ANTIMALWARE APPS ON MOBILE DEVICES

Installing an antimalware program on employees' smart phones, tablets, and laptops not only makes sense, it is also recommended by the Department of Health and Human Services. And since they are the agency that can impose a heavy fine if your organization experiences a data breach, it would be hard to justify ignoring this advice.

HealthIT.gov does not recommend specific antimalware software, but instead says: "Some mobile devices come with security software installed, but you may need to enable the software. If security software does not come installed on your mobile device, you may need to download it. Research the software before downloading to verify it is from a trusted source."[13]

Organizations like AV-Test, an independent IT-security institute, can provide assistance to your search for reliable antimalware software. AV-Test evaluates security apps by exposing them to existing malware to see how well they protect mobile devices, as well as other Windows and Mac machines. Their analysis of mobile security programs for Android phones includes several large and small vendors, including McAfee, Kaspersky, Sophos, Symantec, Playcastle, and Avira, rating each on their ability to detect malware in real time, as well as usability and features. High malware-detection scores went to AhnLab, Avira, Trend Micro, Symantec, and Sophos, among others [14].

Finding reliable antimalware apps for iphones and iPads is much harder. Apple recently removed several anti-malware apps from its Apple store, and currently, the mobile security apps that are available do not protect against viruses, Trojans, and other malware, they help reduce the threat of phishing attacks, they have the ability to wipe the phone of contacts, and can offer assistance in locating a lost phone. Apparently Apple does not see the need for antimalware protection on its phones and tablets, a contention that some security specialists question [15].

There are good antimalware programs available for Apple laptops, however, several of which has also been evaluated by AV-TEST. And contrary to accepted wisdom, Macs can be hacked and can be infected with malware.

BOX B HOW SAFE IS THAT MOBILE APP?

Healthcare professionals, just like the general public, still do not appreciate the risks involved in downloading mobile apps to their phone or tablet. *Apple iOS Security* drives up the point: "While apps provide amazing productivity benefits for users, they also have the potential to negatively impact system security, stability, and user data if they're not handled properly." [16].

It is estimated that at least 16 million mobile devices were infected with malware in 2014. Alcatel-Lucent found that about half of these malware infections occurred on Android phones and tablets because the digital certificates used to authenticate Android apps are less vigorously controlled. "Since Android apps are usually self-signed and can't be traced to the developer, it's easy to hijack Android apps, inject code into them and then re-sign them," according to one *International Business Times* report [17]. (Self-signed means the app developer has not purchased a trust certificate from a Certificate Authority. Some compare self-signing to having a fake driver's license.)

Similarly, another *Forbes* report found 97% of mobile malware is located on Android devices [18]. On the other hand, it is estimated that malware affects less than 1% of other mobile devices, including iPhones, Windows phones, and Blackberries [17].

One of the reasons the statistics are so high for Android phones and tablets is the fact that there are so many of them relative to other brands. Even more relevant to healthcare providers trying to avoid compromised PHI is the fact that most of the infections appear to be coming from unregulated third-party app stores, most of which are located in the Middle East and Asia. The Google Play Store appears to be somewhat more trustworthy.

Several sites that offer Android mobile apps, including Android159 and eoeMarket, did not fare as well as the Google Play store. 33% of the apps coming from Android159 were infected according to the *Forbes* report. EoeMarket, an Android apps store popular in China had a 7% malware penetration.

Many of the threats that creep into Android devices through infected mobile apps would be eliminated if manufacturers and users regularly upgraded their operating systems when a new one became available. After all, one of the reasons technology companies release new versions of their OS is to plug security holes they have discovered in the previous version.

A recent analysis released by Symantec should also make decision makers think twice about allowing Android-based mobile devices to connect to their computer network. The company's 2015 Internet Security Threat Report found 17% of Android apps contained malware, which translates into about 1 million apps. Symantec also discovered the first mobile crypto-ransomware on Android devices. That is a software program that scrambles all the information on your device or network and then refuses to decrypt unless you pay a ransom [19]. On a more positive note, the odds of being infected from an Android-based mobile app are pretty low if users stick to those apps available from Google Play Store.

How low? While a study released by RiskIQ, a cybersecurity company, is somewhat dated and may not reflect any recent improvements to Google's mobile security policy, it does give one reason for pause. RiskIQ found that in 2011 there were about 11,000 apps in the Google Play store that contained malware. By 2013, that number had increased to 42,000. The greatest trouble makers were apps that personalized a person's phone, and entertainment and gaming apps [20].

BYOD: BRING YOUR OWN DISASTER?

CEOs, IT professionals, and secure specialists continue to debate the value and limitations of allowing physicians to bring their own mobile devices into work, the BYOD phenomenon. Many organizations say that it lowers their technology hardware costs, eliminating or reducing the need to buy mobile devices for their clinicians. Many also believe it improves staff productivity. But from a security perspective, BYOD can become a nightmare if not managed correctly.

When I was the Editor of *InformationWeek Healthcare,* I discussed BYOD with Mike Restuccia, the Chief Information Officer at Penn Medicine in Philadelphia. His position was clear: If a physician wants to use her own device in Penn's system, she is "absolutely not allowed" to keep patient data on it [5].

Many healthcare executives take the same position, believing that the risks of allowing PHI on a personally owned tablet or smartphone outweigh the benefits. If you decide to implement the same policy, physicians can still access PHI residing on your hospital or medical practice's in-house servers from their phones and tablets, they just cannot transfer it to their device. Many organizations set things up so that clinicians cannot even do a screen capture of PHI they are viewing on their mobile device—or print it.

One option that allows clinicians to remotely access PHI without storing it on their device is referred to as a "thin client." If you are old enough to remember the days in which computer monitors—or terminals—were all connected to a mainframe computer, you will recall that these terminals were not accompanied by a tower, so they did not have be a hard drive, fan, or other moving parts, just a screen to access the data in the mainframe computer. A thin client is similar to those early terminals.

Of course, the downside here is most clinicians will not want a personal mobile device that only serves as a monitor to read information on your network servers. They want to use the device for other purposes too. And many thin clients do offer more than just a screen to view information located in your organization's in-house computers. Although the terminology varies depending on who you talk to, currently a "zero client" or "ultrathin client" has very little storage capabilities, whereas a thin client has more storage and functionality, allowing the mobile device to carry out some basic tasks on its own. If you are interested in exploring this area of technology, collectively called desktop virtualization, there are many consultants who can provide more details.

MOBILE DEVICE MANAGEMENT SOFTWARE

One option to seriously consider is mobile device management (MDM) software. Several reputable vendors are in this space, including AirWatch, Good Technology, Kaspersky, Sophos, Mobileiron, and Symantec. Many of these tools will even let the user access some of his or her favorite apps but still help keep PHI safe.

MDM programs include a variety of security features, depending on the service you purchase. One is called device "provisioning," which is another way of saying the software controls the type of information that the smartphone or tablet will have access to on your organization's main computers, including specific applications, services, and files. It may also include restricting the mobile apps that each staffer can download onto his or her device. In fact, many healthcare providers will "white list" and "black list" mobile apps based on their reputations and a review of the security threat.

An MDM platform may also limit a member of your staff based on his job description. So if they need to handle financial information, for instance, but do not need to see patients' clinical data, provisioning can restrict access to that information, assuming the pertinent files are organized appropriately.

Other important MDM features include the ability to use the software to remotely lock the mobile device or wipe it of all its content.

MDM programs usually provide a centralized dashboard for administrators to manage all the devices that have access to data on your in-house servers, allowing them to define and enforce your organization's policies and procedures. In practical terms, that means your IT department or consultant can configure all the phones and tablets that have access to your data. They can also send out software updates to all the devices to make sure they have the latest antimalware patches and the latest operating systems.

It is also a good idea to invest in an MDM program that can detect and block mobile devices that have been tampered with, including Apple devices that have been "jailbroken" and Android and Windows phones that are "rooted." Jailbreaking an Apple device is the process by which a user frees it from the limitations imposed by Apple, which subverts the protections on the device that restrict the user to approved software. "Unlocking" refers to freeing the device from the telephone carrier company. Many people use third-party software to do a jailbreak so that they can gain access to mobile apps that Apple has not approved. However, since Apple carefully vets the apps that it allows in its app store, you no longer have the added security that comes from restricting yourself to the Apple security protocols used during that vetting process. (Rooting refers to a similar jailbreaking process on Android and Windows phones.)

Many MDM services also offer the ability to "containerize" or "sandbox" applications and data on the mobile device. The process of sandboxing involves isolating PHI and other sensitive data from personal data on someone's device. The advantage of this feature is it would allow your IT department to wipe the sensitive data from a lost or stolen device without destroying the owner's photos, personal emails, and other valuable information. Do keep in mind, however, that not all MDM programs offer sandboxing, which means that should the need arise to wipe out sensitive information on the mobile device, the user will lose all of that personal data.

Even if you choose not to put a MDM program in place, there are several other security safeguards that HHS encourages healthcare organizations to implement. One of the most important recommendations is to disable any file sharing software or capability. File sharing lets individuals who are on the same network—which includes the internet since it is the biggest network—to connect to each other and trade files. That opens up the possibility of unauthorized persons gaining access to PHI on your device without you knowing about it. It can also allow them to place malware on your system.

Someone on your staff may find it convenient to use a peer-to-peer network (P2P) on their own smartphone to share music or photos with a friend, for instance. That is not a very smart idea for a clinician with patient records on their laptop, tablet or phone—or for anyone else for that matter. Fans of P2P programs may try to downplay the dangers but they are real. In addition, some of these programs run in the background all the time, not just when the file-sharing program window is open. OnGuardOnline.gov brings out: "Some P2P programs open automatically every time you turn on your computer." [6] Unfortunately, there is no single way to disable all the available file-sharing applications in one easy step. It varies depending on the operating system. On an Apple laptop, for instance, it is possible to turn off file sharing in the system preferences window using the "Sharing" icon.

If anyone on your staff is going to be using public Wi-Fi networks, it is also a good idea to enable the firewall and its stealth mode feature if they are on an Apple laptop. That will reduce the odds of attackers even seeing their computer when a staff member is sitting across the room in the local coffee shop. To enable this feature, open the Preferences section, locate the Security icon, click on the firewall option and enable the firewall. (You first need to click the lock icon to unlock this feature and insert your administrator password.) When the firewall is enabled, you can then enable the stealth mode feature in the firewall options section.

On Windows mobile devices, it is also possible to create a measure of "invisibility" while in public places through the Control Panel. The procedure will be slightly different depending on what version of Windows the device is running, but to illustrate the steps, let's use Windows 7.

Once the Control Panel is open, click on the Network and Sharing Center, then the "Choose homegroup and sharing options." Then the Change advanced sharing settings. The mobile device will be less vulnerable to outsiders if you click on the buttons marked:

- Turn off network discovery
- Turn off file and printer sharing
- Turn off public folder sharing

It is also wise to disable media streaming while on a public network. Obviously, you will want to turn this feature back on if you are in a protected private network and need access to video or audio streaming [7]. By the way, after all these security features have been selected, the user has to hit the "save changes" button to enable them. That may seem too obvious to mention but many novices do forget that step.

Another area of concern, especially for anyone bringing a personal mobile device into the workplace, is app downloads. Typically, if you have a MDM program on your hospital or practice computer network, the administrator will vet apps and restrict access to those suspected or known to contain viruses or other malware. But if you are not using MDM, employees need to be very cautious about choosing apps to install on their devices. Some mobile apps will compromise the data on your device or copy your address book or other private data to an external source without your knowledge.

Like any other piece of technology, smartphones, tablets and laptops eventually wear out. Discarding such devices without deleting all the health information is a serious mistake and a breach of HIPAA regulations. Three acceptable options exist:

- Clearing (using software or hardware products to overwrite media with nonsensitive data)
- Purging (degaussing, ie, exposing the media to a strong magnetic field in order to disrupt the recorded magnetic domains)
- Destroying (disintegrating, pulverizing, melting, incinerating, or shredding the media)

The National Institute of Standards and Technology (NIST) offers a detailed guide on how to sanitize data from computers called *Guidelines for Media Sanitization* [8].

As mentioned several times before, staff education is an indispensable part of healthcare security. With that in mind, the Department of Health and Human Services offers several educational tools, including posters, brochures, postcards, and a PowerPoint presentation to help keep mobile security front of mind. The materials are located on the healthit.gov web site [9]. Commercial vendors also have a few helpful tutorials that offer practical advice on keep mobile devices secure, including Verizon [10].

THE VIRTUES OF VIRTUAL PRIVATE NETWORKS

As alluded to earlier in the chapter, a virtual private network (VPN) is a wise decision for a healthcare provider trying to protect PHI. One of the advantages of setting up a VPN is that it bolsters security for mobile device users when they travel, even if it is to a local bagel shop that has Wi-Fi. A VPN has been likened to a secret tunnel that allows users to send private messages and files across a very large public network, usually the Internet. It can connect a mobile user to a practice's or hospital's in-house computers, for instance, or link several offices together, using technology that offers a relative degree of privacy from prying eyes.

Once upon a time, large companies would create a large *actual* private network rather than a virtual one by leasing lines from a telecommunications vendor. This created a physical connection between a home office and a satellite office because it ran cables between the two locations. That is still an option for large healthcare organizations but it is an expensive one. In essence it can link two local area networks (LANs), namely the computer system in your main hospital to a LAN in a second location. Connecting the two LANs creates a wide area network or WAN.

For better and worse, the world now has its own wide area network—the internet. It allows local computer networks to connect at much lower cost, but it does not offer security safeguards so you risk unauthorized persons gaining access to PHI. VPNs provide that security.

VPNs come in two varieties: remote-access VPNs and site-to-site VPNs. Site-to-site VPNs typically connect two or more fixed locations over the internet whereas a remote-access VPN, also called a virtual private dial-up network, will allow remotely located staffers to connect to the main office through an internet service provider. Since this chapter deals with mobile security, we will concentrate on the latter.

To make sense of how these remote access VPNs function, it helps to visualize them and understand a few of their main components.

As Fig. 6.1 shows, the system requires a network access server, also called a media gateway, which is located in your hospital or main medical office. Your remote users—a physician using a tablet, for instance—installs software on his device. This "client" software connects him to the internet, but any data he transmits via the VPN is encapsulated in a secure tunnel. The client software and server also provide the necessary encryption to keep the transmission isolated from the rest of the traffic coursing through the internet.

Depending on the VPN system you choose to use and the type of mobile devices your staff has, you may already have the client software built into the device. The iPhone 6, for instance, has the software available from its Settings screen. That software would then connect to a network access server that is located at your main headquarters.

The security provided by a VPN system involves a complex system of encryption, hiding packets of data within other packets of data, and a variety of security

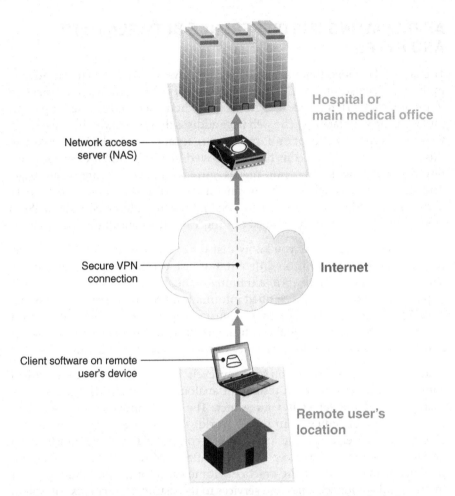

Hospital or
main medical office

Network access
server (NAS)

Secure VPN
connection

Internet

Client software on remote
user's device

Remote user's
location

FIGURE 6.1 The path taken by patient information as it moves through a virtual private network.

protocols, including IPSec, PPP, SSL, and others. Suffice it to say, these technical tools reduce the risk of unauthorized persons gaining access to PHI.

Circling back to the recommendations from the Department of Health and Human Services on using mobile devices, in a tutorial on wireless communication, the government poses the rhetorical question: "How should you access health information using your smartphone, tablet or laptop when you are in a public space? Use a virtual private network or VPN..." [11] If your organization does experience a data breach and an OCR investigator comes visiting to determine what happened, having a VPN in place is one less opportunity for blame to be placed at your doorstep.

APPRECIATING THE DIFFERENCE BETWEEN HTTP AND HTTPS

The same HHS video that recommends using a VPN to secure PHI also advises mobile device users to look for a secure browser connection when connecting to the internet. (That advice also holds true when you are using desktop computers inside your facility.) The web page address that appears at the top of each web page is called a URL or uniform resource locator. When the URL looks like this: https://www.hipaa.com/hipaa-protected-health-information-what-does-phi-include/, that "s" after http means you are viewing a more secure page. And that privacy is achieved by means of a set of rules—a "protocol" in IT parlance—called Secure Sockets Layer (SSL). Knowing a few basics about SSL is worth your time as a decision maker hiring a security consultant or employee.

If you work in healthcare, you know that it has its own specialized language. Information technology is no different, but just as frustrating for outsiders to decipher. In *CISSP Training Kit,* a training manual to prepare IT professionals to pass the test to become a certified information systems security professional (CISSP), the author offers a rather confusing explanation of SSL—at least for laypersons: "SSL uses a digital certificate to authenticate the web-based server to the client and then performs secure symmetric session key distribution."[12]

That sentence is bewildering on so many levels: The terms client and server will confuse computer novices. A restaurant analogy might help. The client is the customer, and the server is your waiter. The server provides the meal and the customer consumes it. In the IT world, that analogy applies to various situations. The server can be a specialized computer that looks much like a desktop computer tower, except with specialized software and hardware components. It may reside in the practice's home office or hospital building—or in the cloud—and feeds files and services to its customers or clients. The client can be a desktop computer or mobile device that "consumes" the information, taking advantage of the data residing on that specialized computer, either through a wired connection or wireless network.

In the quote cited previously, we have a web server, which might be a computer located a Wal-Mart's headquarters and which houses the web site's content—picture of clothing, video clips, an ordering apparatus and so on. The client can be the Internet Explorer or Safari web browser on your laptop. When you request to see content on the Wal-Mart web site, the web server serves up web pages by sending them over the internet to the browser application on your laptop.

Over the years, this client/web server relationship has become rather unsafe, with malware existing on all sorts of web pages. It used to be web surfers were warned to avoid esoteric or unconventional web sites for fear they were infected-sites such as Marty's Medical Miracles or Fanny's Fantasies. But these days, even reputable organizations like Reuters, Yahoo, and Youtube have been victimized. Antimalware software helps to catch many of these problems. And vendors like Symantec offer a "safe browsing" feature that helps detect dangerous sites within a Google search results list. But things still fall through the cracks.

SSL is one more weapon in this arsenal of protective services. As the aforementioned quote indicates, it makes use of a digital certificate to authenticate the web server. The owner of a web site buys one or more of these certificates from a company—called a Certificate Authority. Basically they are buying a very long string of computer code that acts as a lock. It creates an encrypted channel between the client—the web browser on a physician's tablet, for instance—and the server—the log-in page for a web site such as UpToDate.

If you "looked behind the curtain" at the log-in page for UpToDate—a well-respected clinical reference database—you would notice the statement "The identity of this web site has been verified by Symantec Class 3 secure server CA-GA.... The connection is encrypted using....." The encryption makes use of a digital key; it is called symmetric encryption because it uses a private key to allow the sender to encrypt the patient data; the same key is used by the recipient to decrypt the data.

You will notice that I refer to SSL as *one more weapon* in the arsenal. Using a SSL certified web site alone does not guarantee that the PHI you send across the Internet is impossible to steal. But when combined with all the other safeguards discussed in the book, it creates a multilayered approach that reduces the likelihood of a data breach. Security specialists like to use the term Defense in Depth to describe the approach. No single measure will create an impenetrable fortress but stacking layer upon layer of protections is a lot like using several security measures to keep burglars out of your home. If you add bolt locks, door knob locks, security cameras, guard dogs, and a security alarm system in your home, these measures may not prevent a professional thief from breaking in, but if he sees a much-less-protected house down the street with equally valuable treasure, it is likely he will take the path of least resistance.

References

[1] C.E. Ventola, Mobile Devices and Apps for Health Care Professionals: Uses and Benefits, Pharm. Ther. 39 (5) (2014) 356–364 http://www.ncbi.nlm.nih.gov/pmc/articles/PMC4029126/.

[2] HHS Office of Civil Rights. Guidance to render unsecured protected health information unusable, unreadable, or indecipherable to unauthorized individuals. http://www.hhs.gov/ocr/privacy/hipaa/administrative/breachnotificationrule/brguidance.html.

[3] Healthit.gov. Tips to protect and secure health information. http://www.healthit.gov/providers-professionals/10-use-adequate-security-send-or-receive-health-information-over-public-wi-f.

[4] P. Cerrato. How your own laptop or smartphone can wreak havoc at work. Medscape Business of Medicine. http://www.medscape.com/viewarticle/779829, 2013.

[5] P. Cerrato. Why BYOD doesn't always work in healthcare, InformationWeek DARKReading. http://www.darkreading.com/risk-management/why-byod-doesnt-always-work-in-healthcare/d/d-id/1103076, 2012.

[6] OnGuardOnline.gov. P2P file-sharing risks. http://www.onguardonline.gov/p2p.

[7] Microsoft. Privacy and security when streaming your media: frequently asked questions. http://windows.microsoft.com/en-us/windows7/privacy-and-security-when-streaming-your-media-frequently-asked-questions.

[8] National Institute of Standards and Technology. Guidelines for media sanitization. http://nvlpubs.nist.gov/nistpubs/SpecialPublications/NIST.SP.800-88r1.pdf, 2014.

[9] HealthIT.gov. Mobile device privacy and security: downloadable materials. http://www.healthit.gov/providers-professionals/downloadable-materials.

[10] Verizon Wireless. 8 Common-sense tips to keep your smartphone secure. http://www.verizonwireless.com/mobile-living/network-and-plans/security-app-tips-to-keep-your-smartphone-secure/.

[11] HealthIT.gov. Can you protect patients' health information when using a public Wi-Fi network? Mobile Health Sevurity and Accessing a Public Wi-Fi Nework. http://www.healthit.gov/providers-professionals/can-you-protect-patients-health-information-when-using-public-wi-fi-network.

[12] D.R. Miller, CISSP Training Kit, Microsoft Press, Redmond, WA, (2014) p. 483.

[13] HealthIT.gov. Install and enable security software. http://www.healthit.gov/providers-professionals/6-install-and-enable-security-software.

[14] AV TEST. The best antivirus software for Android. https://www.av-test.org/en/antivirus/mobile-devices/android/, 2015.

[15] TrendMicro. Revisiting iOS security as Apple cracks down on antimalware apps. http://www.trendmicro.com/vinfo/us/security/news/mobile-safety/revisiting-ios-security-as-apple-cracks-down-on-antimalware-apps, 2015.

[16] Apple. iOS Security White Paper. https://www.apple.com/business/docs/iOS_Security_Guide.pdf, 2015.

[17] Russon M. 16 million mobile devices infected by malware in 2014 with hacking attempts on the rise, International Business Times. http://www.ibtimes.co.uk/16-million-mobile-devices-infected-by-malware-2014-hacking-attempts-rise-1488367, 2015.

[18] G. Kelly. Report: 97% of mobile malware is on Android, This is the easy way you stay safe. http://www.forbes.com/sites/gordonkelly/2014/03/24/report-97-of-mobile-malware-is-on-android-this-is-the-easy-way-you-stay-safe/, 2014.

[19] D. Tynan. Report: 1 in 5 Android apps is malware, Yahoo Tech. https://www.yahoo.com/tech/report-one-in-five-android-apps-is-malware-117202610899.html, 2015.

[20] Z. Miners. Report: malware-infected Android apps spike in the Google Play store, PCWORLD.http://www.pcworld.com/article/2099421/report-malwareinfected-android-apps-spike-in-the-google-play-store.html, 2014.

CHAPTER 7

Medical Device Security

Medical device security remains one of the most challenging and contentious areas to manage. Device manufacturers insist that hospitals and medical practices keep their hands off the inner workings of their products while providers complain that the technology inside the devices is too often out of date and thus vulnerable to attack, or impossible to update with the latest antimalware patches.

Although provider organizations have legitimate concerns about the lack of security of medical devices, playing the blame game is counterproductive. The top priority of device manufacturers is patient safety/device functionality, not the ability of their devices to be securely linked to a hospital's computer network. They take this responsibility seriously because they realize that corrupted software or hardware in an IV pump, heart defibrillator, or blood gas analyzer can kill patients.

Sean P, Murphy, a respected healthcare security specialist, sums up the dilemma this way: "Unlike other computing device manufacturers, medical device manufacturers retain a great deal of responsibility for their devices even after they are sold …The reason for this has to do with safety rather than cybersecurity, and this responsibility can actually introduce security risks. Because medical devices are FDA-regulated and patient safety is a concern, medical device manufacturers must test and approve all third party software before a healthcare organization can update a medical device. This process can, at best, delay the software vulnerability patch management process; at worst, it can cause medical devices to remain unpatched and vulnerable to exploit on the hospital LAN [local access network]." [1]

That said, patient safety and network security don't have to be mutually exclusive priorities. With adequate communication and cooperation between device manufacturers and providers, it should be possible to keep both patients *and* hospital/practice servers safe from harm. After all, allowing devices to remain unprotected from cyberattack in itself poses a threat to patient safety, either by allowing malware to corrupt patient records, or directly disrupting the function of an infected device.

HOW REAL IS THE THREAT?

Some business executives and physicians may be skeptical about the risks posed by medical devices. Is this paranoia? Consider the evidence to date: In 2011, Jay Radcliffe, a computer security researcher, demonstrated that he could hack into a Medtronic insulin pump and gain remote control of the device. Since then, Barnaby Jack, another security specialist, has shown he can cause some medication pumps to deliver fatal insulin doses from up to 300 feet away [2].

In 2010, a Veterans Affairs catheterization lab in New Jersey had to close down temporarily because its computerized devices were infected with malware. Similarly, William Maisel, deputy director of science and chief scientist for FDA Center for Devices and Radiological Health has stated that the FDA is "aware of hundreds of medical devices that have been infected by malware.... It is not difficult to imagine how these types of events could lead to patient harm." [3]

More recently, in July 2015, both the US Department of Homeland Security and FDA warned hospitals not to use a Hospira Symbiq infusion pump because of a security vulnerability that allows hackers to gain remote control of the system. And John Halamka, MD, CIO at Beth Israel Deaconess Medical Center (BIDMC) in Boston, has reported a breach that had to be reported to federal authorities that involved a medical device. As he explained the account, the breach occurred "when a medical device manufacturer removed our hospital provided security protections in order to update a device from the Internet. It took about 30 seconds for the unprotected device to become infected and transmit data over the Internet. The Office of Civil Rights adjudicated that it was the manufacturer, not BIDMC, which was responsible for the breach. We were advised to follow any visiting manufacturer reps around the hospital to ensure that they do not remove hospital provided security protections in the future." [4]

In a separate incident, hackers were able to insert malware in surgical blood gas analyzers at an unnamed hospital. That gave them a way to sneak into the facility's computer network and locate passwords, and obtain sensitive data [5]. The list of medical device-related data breaches and infections at healthcare organizations goes on and on.

TAKING A CLOSER LOOK AT THE "PATHOLOGY" BEHIND MEDJACKING

The phenomenon has become commonplace enough to earn its own distinct term: "Medjacking," short for medical device hijacking. One reason for these breaches is the out of date operating systems (OS) still being used in many devices, including Windows 2000 and XP. The problem with old operating systems is the software companies that created them stop supporting them, which means they also stop issuing security patches, which in turn makes them an easy target for hackers. In effect, they become low hanging fruit that is much more appetizing and much less work than breaking into a computer with an OS that is regularly upgraded. (Stephen Warren, former IO for the U.S. Department of Veterans Affairs, recently pointed out that if you connect a medical device to a computer running Windows XP to the Internet, expect it to be compromised in 7 seconds.) [6]

Outdated operating systems become even more problematic if device manufacturers do not allow IT professionals working for a hospital or medical practice to gain access to the device so they can devise a way to protect it. At the very least, device makers should be giving healthcare providers enough information about the connectivity of the products so that it is possible for hospitals and practices to create customized firewalls and other security measures that would mitigate the risk of unauthorized persons gaining access to an organization's computer network. John Halamka, for instance, has often asked device makers to provide a map of network ports and protocols that their products use to communicate with a hospital servers, without much success.

As you may recall from my earlier explanation of how firewalls work, they are hardware and/or software that serves as the first line of defense, offering a measure of protection by blocking suspicious traffic from the internet. One common approach to firewall management is to have a packet filter take a "guilty until proven innocent" position, in which it blocks all traffic by default. Then the IT team adds rules (called protocols) that include exceptions to this default to allow selected information to pass through. If a device manufacturer gives your IT team enough detail about its ports and protocols—in other words, how someone can gain entry into the device's inner workings—your IT department can design a firewall that only allows access through those virtual ports and protocols.

Another option is for device makers to take the lead in regularly updating the software on the machines with the latest antimalware patches and other security defenses. Of course, that adds to their costs and without a direct mandate or clearly written federal regulations demanding such measures, some companies are disinclined to take action.

Enter the FDA, the agency that is directly responsible for medical device regulation.

WHAT IS THE FDA DOING?

The agency, recognizing the growing threat to healthcare organizations that incorporate medical devices into their computer networks, recently issued a set of non-binding recommendations, *Guidance for Industry – Cybersecurity for Networked Medical Devices Containing Off-the-Shelf (OTS) Software* [7]. In answer to the question: Who is responsible for ensuring the safety and effectiveness of medical devices that incorporate OTS software? FDA states: "You (the device manufacturer who uses OTS software in your medical device) bear the responsibility for the continued safe and effective performance of the medical device, including the performance of OTS software that is part of the device."

What exactly does that responsibility entail? The agency says the device manufacturer needs to be vigilant and responsive to cybersecurity vulnerabilities. And that responsibility is part of the obligation spelled out in federal regulation 21 CFR 820.100. However, when asked by providers to maintain up-to-date security patches, some manufacturers have resisted, claiming that to do so would require them to obtain recertification from FDA before the device could be put back on the market. But the aforementioned *Guidance* document clearly states that that is not usually required.

The FDA guidelines specifically ask the question: "Is FDA premarket review required prior to implementation of a software patch to address a cybersecurity vulnerability?" The answer: "Usually not."

To make sense of this "Usually not" answer, it helps to first understand the types of devices that require FDA clearance or approval. Medical devices that receive the agency's blessing through its 510(k) mechanism are "cleared" by the agency after it reviews the manufacturer's application; in these cases the device is substantially equivalent to a device that is already legally marketed for the same use. Devices that do not fall into that category may require a premarket approval application (PMA), in which case the company has to prove that its product is safe and effective.

The FDA cybersecurity guidelines explain that it would only be necessary to give a new 510(k) submission to FDA if either (1) the device has a new or changed indication for use—for instance, the company wants to sell the device for use in a different disease, or (2) the proposed change in the device could significantly affect the safety or effectiveness of the device. With that second possibility in mind, the agency states: "It is possible, but unlikely, that a software patch will need a new 510(k) submission."

With regard to medical devices that were approved through a premarket approval application, the same criteria apply when considering the need for a PMS supplement. "Otherwise, you [the device manufacturer] should report your decision to apply a software patch to your PMA device to FDA in your annual reports."

The agency is also encouraging closer collaboration between device makers, the end users, and the technology companies that provide the off-the-shelf software that they are installing in their units. That is really the best way the devices can hope to resist hacker invasions. And although the device makers are usually the ones to install any security updates, there will be times when they need to get the hospital and/or software maker involved.

Here we enter a tricky area since the device manufacturer is ultimately answerable for any patient safety issues that may arise. Nonetheless, the *Guideline* states:

> While it is customary for the medical device manufacturer to perform these software maintenance activities, there may be situations in which it is appropriate for the user facility, OTS vendor, or a third party to be involved. Your software maintenance plan should provide a mechanism for you to exercise overall responsibility while delegating specific tasks to other parties. The vast majority of healthcare organizations will lack detailed design information and technical resources to assume primary maintenance responsibility for medical device software and, therefore, will rely on you to assume the primary maintenance responsibility.

Unfortunately for hospitals and medical practices, the FDA guidelines do not carry the force of law, so manufacturers that find them too burdensome and too expensive to implement will likely ignore them. It is times like this when working with large device manufacturers with deep pockets makes the most sense.

On a more positive note, the future looks brighter. The FDA advice on strengthening cybersecurity in *new* devices that have yet to receive clearance or approval should have a significant impact on the industry. While the guidelines are not binding, ignoring them could result in delayed or denied approval [8].

The list of recommendations from the FDA reads like the syllabus from a Security 101 course: [9]

- Limit access to devices through the authentication of users (eg, user ID and password, smartcard, biometric)
- Use automatic timed methods to terminate sessions within the system where appropriate for the use environment
- Where appropriate, employ a layered authorization model by differentiating privileges on the basis of the user's role (eg, caregiver, system administrator) or device role
- Use appropriate authentication (eg, multifactor authentication to permit privileged device access to system administrators, service technicians, maintenance personnel)
- Strengthen password protection by avoiding "hardcoded" password or common words (ie, passwords which are the same for each device, difficult to change, and vulnerable to public disclosure) and limit public access to passwords used for privileged device access;
- Where appropriate, provide physical locks on devices and their communication ports to minimize tampering
- Require user authentication or other appropriate controls before permitting software or firmware updates, including those affecting the operating system, applications, and anti-malware

- Restrict software or firmware updates to authenticated code. One authentication method manufacturers may consider is code signature verification
- Use systematic procedures for authorized users to download version-identifiable software and firmware from the manufacturer
- Ensure capability of secure data transfer to and from the device, and when appropriate, use methods for encryption
- Implement features that allow for security compromises to be detected, recognized, logged, timed, and acted upon during normal use
- Develop and provide information to the end user concerning appropriate actions to take upon detection of a cybersecurity event
- Implement device features that protect critical functionality, even when the device's cybersecurity has been compromised
- Provide methods for retention and recovery of device configuration by an authenticated privileged user

FDA is not to only federal agency concerned about the security holes in medical devices. On September 10, 2015, the Federal Bureau of Investigation issued a public service announcement entitled: "Internet Of Things Poses Opportunities For Cyber Crime," further emphasizing that said risks are not to be taken lightly [10]. The FBI's concerns, however, go beyond traditional medical devices and include HVAC remotes, security systems, appliances like smart TVs, office equipment including printers, Wi-Fi cameras, fuel monitoring systems, entertainment devices to control music or TV from a mobile device, thermostats, and any type of wearable device. Basically the Bureau is including any device or object that connects to the Internet to automatically send and receive data.

The FBI is especially concerned about devices that have built-in default passwords or open Wi-Fi connections, which are easy targets for cyber criminals to access a hospital or medical practice's computer network, assuming of course that the devices are connected to the network. It advises users to change default passwords ASAP because hackers often obtain these codes by searching the internet. With access to default passwords, hackers can then assign themselves as the administrator of the device or system, and do all sorts of mischief, including deactivating alarm systems, opening doors, recording audio and video, and obtaining sensitive patient information. As you may recall from an earlier chapter, allowing unauthorized persons to gain physical access to a building or room containing protected health information is a HIPAA violation.

It is also possible for criminals to gain access to unprotected medical devices used in home health care. If those units are used to send and receive data from your healthcare organization, your network is once again vulnerable. Even more important, manipulating the functionality of the home health device can endanger patient's health.

Finally the Bureau provided a list of recommendations to help shore up the security of internet of Things (IoT) devices, many of which are similar to the advice offered by FDA:

- Isolate IoT devices on their own protected networks
- Disable UPnP on routers; Universal Plug and Play protocol refers to the process by which devices remotely connect and communicate with a network without authentication. UPnP is designed to self-configure when attached to an IP address, making it vulnerable to exploitation
- Consider whether IoT devices are ideal for their intended purpose
- Purchase IoT devices from manufacturers with a track record of providing secure devices
- When available, update IoT devices with security patches
- Be aware of the capabilities of the devices and appliances installed in homes and businesses. If a device comes with a default password or an open Wi-Fi connection, change the password and only allow it to operate on a network with a secured Wi-Fi router
- Use current best practices when connecting IoT devices to wireless networks, and when connecting remotely to an IoT device
- Patients should be informed about the capabilities of any medical devices prescribed for at-home use. If the device is capable of remote operation or transmission of data, it could be a target for a malicious actor
- Ensure all default passwords are changed to strong passwords. Do not use the default password determined by the device manufacturer. Many default passwords can be easily located on the internet. Do not use common words and simple phrases or passwords containing easily obtainable personal information, such as important dates or names of children or pets. If the device does not allow the capability to change the access password, ensure the device providing wireless Internet service has a strong password and uses strong encryption

DEALING WITH EXISTING MEDICAL DEVICE VULNERABILITIES

In an ideal world, security safeguards outlined by FDA and FBI should have already been in place several years ago, before healthcare data breaches became so commonplace. Since that never occurred, your organization is now faced with the very real problem of purchasing and managing existing medical devices with all their security flaws.

If your hospital, clinic, or practice is considering a device purchase, the first place to start is with the Manufacturer Disclosure Statement for Medical Device Security or MDS[2]. The form is a means by which the device maker outlines security-related features of the products they manufacture. Insisting that device manufacturers provide the completed form as part of the Request for Proposal and purchasing process is a good business practice. The statement will help your team more easily compare security features across different devices and different manufacturers, which in turn allows you to get a better sense of which companies' security protocols align best with security policies and security safeguards already in place in your facility.

The MDS^2 form was initially created by the Healthcare Information Management Systems Society (HIMSS) and the American College of Clinical Engineering. It was later standardized when HIMSS and the National Electrical Manufacturers Association joined forces. The form helps providers assess and address the vulnerabilities and risks associated with each device. Among the issues delineated in the MDS^2 form is information on maintaining and storing ePHI, backing up data, installing security patches, remote service access, and audit logs that document access to ePHI.

HOW ARE MEDICAL DEVICE COMPANIES COPING?

Although many providers have had problems getting manufacturers to shore up device security, that is not to suggest that device makers are indifferent about these issues. In fact, several have been investigating device vulnerabilities and attempting to keep customers informed.

Philips Healthcare, for instance, posts a web page in which it outlines security advisories and provides archives. As we went to press, the company had listed advisories on the Unix Shellshock vulnerability, a group of security bugs that can allow attackers to gain unauthorized access to a computer network. It also alerted customers about the possibility that an SSLv3 security vulnerability and the so-called "Heartbleed" bug may affect medical devices, stating that "The effect of this vulnerability on Philips healthcare products and services is being investigated by the Philips engineering and product security teams…; This site will be updated once a solution is available for any affected product(s)."

The vendor has also notified device users that Microsoft is no longer providing support for its Windows XP operating system, which means any medical devices that were built on XP are vulnerable to attack because Microsoft is no longer pushing out security updates. Philips goes on to explain that "Where feasible, Philips Healthcare has been developing solutions for products running Windows XP to address continuity of protection against known and emerging security threats and vulnerabilities. To this end, Philips Healthcare will provide product-specific Statements to assist customers. Where applicable, these Product Statements may provide upgrade or field change order information." [11] More details on how the company works with hospitals and practices to reduce the risk of a security incident are available in its Product Security Policy Statement [12].

FIRMING UP THE FIRMWARE

One of the problems facing device manufacturers large and small is flawed firmware. Firmware is s specific type of software embedded in a variety of electronic devices including consumer appliances, digital watches, traffic lights—and many medical devices. It is a set of instructions that tells the device how to communicate with computer hardware. It is called firmware because it is designed to be left unaltered by end users—unless it needs to be updated. Because it is not usually designed to be altered by customers, the devices are not typically equipped with a keyboard to rewrite the code.

In 2013, security researchers uncovered hard-coded password vulnerabilities in hundreds of medical devices from about 40 vendors, prompting the US Department of Homeland Security to issue an advisory to manufacturers about the problem [13]. The same advisory explained that the affected devices include surgical and anesthesia devices, ventilators, drug infusion pumps, external defibrillators, patient monitors, and laboratory and analysis equipment manufactured by a broad range of companies. Although that advisory was issued in 2013, there is little doubt that infected and/or vulnerable firmware continues to be a security threat to healthcare organizations. Making matters worse, Terry Dunlap, a managing partner with Tactical Network Solutions, points out that many device manufacturers outsource the creation of their firmware. The problem with that tactic is it can leave the device manufacturer in the dark as to the security risks inherent in the firmware's computer code. It might also explain why some are unable to provide guidance to hospitals and medical practices trying to build firewalls that prevent hackers from gaining access to their computer network through the medical device.

A case in point: In a recent blog on medical device security, John Halamka states:

> Over the past few years, I've asked medical device manufacturers to give me a precise map of the network ports and protocols used by their devices so that I can build a "pinpoint" firewall – only allowing the minimum necessary transactions from/to the device. Many manufacturers do not seem to know the minimum necessary communication requirements for their products.

If in fact, a device manufacturer has not designed the firmware code in its product from the ground up, it would come as no surprise to discover that it does not know enough about the communication requirements needed to safely connect the device to a hospital's network. As you may recall from my earlier explanation on how firewalls work, one of the things they do is block certain virtual communication ports and allow others. Each port has a number and set of rules on how to communicate with it. If the device maker can tell a hospital which ports it uses to connect to the hospital network, then an engineer or analyst can block the unnecessary ports—weak ports that are easy for hackers to penetrate.

Tactical Network Solutions and Klocwork are among a few specialized vendors that analyze firmware in electronic devices to find security weaknesses. During attendance at a recent FDA workshop, Dunlap says he had occasion to discuss the value of firmware analysis to detect vulnerabilities with several manufacturers. The manufacturers' resistance to such analyses focused on liability. Essentially they were saying: "It is not mandated. And if we know about it ahead of time and something happens, we are legally liable."

Awareness of such resistance provides valuable intelligence to any healthcare provider as it enters the procurement process and entertains vendor proposals. One obvious question you want answered: Has your embedded software been fully vetted to detect possible security holes. Obviously, no analysis can turn a medical device into an impenetrable fortress, but there are several vulnerabilities that should be checked. They include hard-coded passwords, buffer overflows, and open virtual ports.

If you have any doubts about the vulnerabilities inherent in firmware, a 2014 report entitled "A Large-Scale Analysis of the Security of Embedded Firmwares" should put those doubts to rest. Andrei Costin and colleagues from Usenix, the Advanced Computing Sciences Association, found 38 previously unknown vulnerabilities in 693 firmware images. In total, they concluded that these weaknesses affect at least 140,000 devices accessible over the Internet. (Their analysis was not limited to medical devices.) [14]

Many of these weaknesses are preventable as a recent case report from Klocwork illustrates. During development of a prosthetic arm that replaces a human limb, the company worked with the software teams at Johns Hopkins University's Applied Physics Lab. Klocwork's analysis of the embedded software detected potentially harmful security vulnerabilities that could allow hackers to "access the system's communication protocol to cause system failure or inject malicious code." [15] Many similar firmware defects would likely be detected if more developers and manufacturers were willing in invest in this type of analysis early on.

ARE MEDICAL DEVICE MANUFACTURERS HIPAA ACCOUNTABLE?

Although some of the device vendors that Terry Dunlap spoke with believe they are not liable for a data breach that results from a defect in their product's software, that position is questionable. Device manufacturers typically enter into formal agreements with hospitals and practices, often establishing themselves officially as "business associates" (BAs). That designation carries with it certain obligations as outlined in HIPAA and HITECH.

In the original HIPAA regulations, first enacted in 1996, BAs were not considered liable if a data breach that exposed protected health information occurred as a result of their lax security measures. The Omnibus Final Rule of 2013, ushered in with the Health Information Technology for Economic and Clinical Health Act (HITECH), changed all that. BAs now share the responsibilities with "covered entities," including hospitals and other healthcare organizations, to keep patient data secure.

The law firm Sheppard Mullin explains the matter clearly. A device manufacturer has to weigh three factors when trying to determine whether the patient data collected on its machine is subject to HIPAA and HITECH regulations:

- "Does the information qualify as Protected Health Information?
- Is a Covered Entity involved?
- Does a Business Associate relationship exist with a Covered Entity?" [16] [Sheppard]

To be considered PHI, the data contained in the device needs to be individually identifiable health information. A covered entity, as defined in the regulations, includes (1) healthcare providers, namely doctors, clinics, psychologists, dentists, chiropractors, nursing homes, and pharmacies, (2) health plans, which include health insurance companies, HMOs, company health plans, and government programs such as Medicare and Medicaid, and (3) healthcare clearinghouses. HIPAA defines a BA as "a person or entity that performs certain functions or activities that involve the use or disclosure of protected health information on behalf of, or provides services to, a covered entity." Many device makers will meet all three of the aforementioned criteria and therefore will share accountability, which means they need to take all reasonable measures to mitigate the risk of a data breach [17].

WEIGHING YOUR SECURITY OPTIONS

Even if you are working with a cooperative device manufacturer and you have worked out a shared strategy, your facility will still need its own plan of action to bolster security. As mentioned previously, the FDA and FBI provide several practical recommendations. You may also want to look to other organizations for best practices.

The US Department of Veterans Affairs has developed a Medical Device Isolation Architecture that is worth a closer look. Effective governance is an important component of the VA's approach. Like many IT managers, Stephen Warren, the agency's former CIO, used a defense in depth strategy that divides the responsibility for keeping medical devices safe among two main groups, making sure nothing slips through the cracks between them. Warren's IT team protects the devices "at the boundaries" while the agency's biomedical staff works to keep the individual devices working securely in each facility.

Equally important, Warren and his associates focused their efforts on one of the weakest links in any security chain: People. The agency has found that device vendors all too often have their technicians insert USB drives into the machines to update software or service the devices. In the process, they bypass laptops that the VA has put in place to scan USB drives for malware. Additionally, the agency watches these outside technicians to make certain they are not accessing the Internet through a device's network connectivity. Similarly, VA staffers are forbidden from surfing the Internet through medical devices [18].

Finally, as you and your IT consultants or staffers consider fortifying medical device security, you will want to review a report issued by the Deloitte Center for Health Solutions. Deloitte, one of the largest consulting groups in the world, interviewed several specialists in information security, clinical engineering, and compliance to glean recommendations. Like many other experts in the field, they emphasized the need for "robust governance, risk identification, and risk management."

The Deloitte analysis also drew attention to the recent FDA guidelines that outlined the need for strong cybersecurity during the premarket approval process, pointing out "the need for medical device manufacturers to produce evidence that their risk assessment process (as outlined in ISO 14971:2007) considered both 'intentional' and unintentional security risks to the medical device and addressed those risks with appropriate security controls as part of the device's design." [19] And once again, the importance of cooperation and collaboration was emphasized in the Deloitte report: "Manufacturers also should consider collaborating with their customers' clinical engineers and physicians to develop a catalog of use cases from which security vulnerabilities can be derived specific to their medical device and its intended use."

References

[1] S.A. Murphy, Healthcare Information Security and Privacy, McGraw Hill Education, New York, 2015, p. 233.

[2] B. Buntz. Medtech security researcher joins forces with FDA, Qmed. http://www.qmed.com/news/medtech-security-researcher-joins-forces-fda, 2013.

[3] L. Husten. FDA raises concerns about the cybersecurity of medical devices, Forbes.com. http://www.forbes.com/sites/larryhusten/2013/06/18/fda-raises-concerns-about-the-cybersecurity-of-medical-devices/, 2013.

[4] J. Halamka. The security of medical devices, Life as a Healthcare CIO. http://geekdoctor.blogspot.com/2015/08/the-security-of-medical-devices.html, 2015.

[5] J. Enriquez. Medjacking: how hackers use medical devices to launch cyber attacks, Med Device Online. http://www.meddeviceonline.com/doc/medjacking-how-hackers-use-medical-devices-to-launch-cyber-attacks-0001, 2015.

[6] B. Eastwood. 5 ways to close common medical device vulnerabilities, FierceHealthIT. http://www.fiercehealthit.com/story/5-ways-close-common-medical-device-vulnerabilities/2015-05-08, 2015.

[7] [FDA1] FDA. Guidance for industry cybersecurity for networked medical devices containing off-the-shelf (OTS) software. http://www.fda.gov/downloads/MedicalDevices/DeviceRegulationandGuidance/GuidanceDocuments/ucm077823.pdf, 2015.

[8] P. Desjardins. FDA scrutinizes networked medical device security, InformationWeek Healthcare. http://www.informationweek.com/healthcare/security-and-privacy/fda-scrutinizes-networked-medical-device-security/a/d-id/1317758, 2014.

[9] FDA. Content of premarket submissions for management of cybersecurity in medical devices guidance for industry and Food and Drug Administration Staff. http://www.fda.gov/downloads/MedicalDevices/DeviceRegulationandGuidance/GuidanceDocuments/UCM356190.pdf, 2014.

[10] Federal Bureau of Investigation. Internet of things poses opportunities for cyber crime. http://www.ic3.gov/media/2015/150910.aspx, 2015.

[11] Philips Healthcare. Security status. http://www.usa.philips.com/healthcare/about/customer-support/product-security.

[12] Philips Healthcare. Product Security Policy Statement. http://www.usa.philips.com/b-dam/b2bhc/us/whitepapers/support/Product_Security_Policy_Statement_Aug_2011.pdf, 2011.

[13] US Department of Homeland Security. Alert (ICS-ALERT-13-164-01) medical devices hard-coded passwords. https://ics-cert.us-cert.gov/alerts/ICS-ALERT-13-164-01, 2013.

[14] A. Costin, J. Zaddach, et al. A large-scale analysis of the security of embedded firmwares. This paper is included in the Proceedings of the 23rd USENIX Security Symposium, San Diego, CA, August 20–22, 2014. https://www.usenix.org/system/files/conference/usenixsecurity14/sec14-paper-costin.pdf, 2014.

[15] Klocwork. Case Study: DARPA, Enhancing software reliability and developer productivity while building the next generation of human prosthetics. http://www.klocwork.com/getattachment/3db34ee2-9378-4019-bfd5-28eaf1271921/Enhancing-Software-Reliability-Johns-Hopkins?sitename=Klocwork.

[16] S. Mullin. HIPAA/HITECH compliance strategies for medical device manufacturers, FDA Law Update. http://www.fdalawblog.com/2013/08/articles/legislation/hipaahitech-compliance-strategies-for-medical-device-manufacturers/, 2013.

[17] R. Rose. How does HIPAA and the HITECH Act impact medical device and pharma companies? Health IT and CIO Review. http://www.beckershospitalreview.com/healthcare-information-technology/how-does-hipaa-and-the-hitech-act-impact-medical-device-and-pharma-companies.html, 2013.

[18] M.K. McGee. How VA keeps medical devices clean, Healthcare Info Security. http://www.healthcareinfosecurity.com/blogs/how-va-keeps-medical-devices-clean-p-1864, 2015.

[19] Deloitte Center for Health Solutions. Issue brief: networked medical device cybersecurity and patient safety: Perspectives of health care information cybersecurity executives. http://www2.deloitte.com/content/dam/Deloitte/us/Documents/risk/us-risk-networked-medical-device-11102014.pdf, 2013.

CHAPTER 8

Educating Medical and Administrative Staff

The need to train medical and administrative staff members has been mentioned several times in chapter 2: How Well Protected in Your Protected Health Information? Perception Versus Reality. The federal government's regulations require it and common sense demands it.

More specifically, 45CFR 164.308 (a)(5)(i) says "Standard: Security awareness and training. Implement a security awareness and training program for all members of its workforce (including management)." [1] Elsewhere, the regulations state that: "A covered entity must train all members of its work force on the policies and procedures with respect to PHI ..., as necessary and appropriate for the members of the work force to carry out their function within the covered entity." [2] If you are a hospital, medical practice, healthcare clearinghouse, or a business associate of any of these organizations, the government considers you a covered entity. The rules also require you to document the fact that the staff training has occurred.

There are several public and commercially available training materials available to help your organization meet these requirements, but before I go into detail on what needs to be covered during training and discuss some of the available resources, let's step back and look at the bigger picture first.

CULTURE BEFORE EDUCATION

All the training in the world will do little good if it falls on deaf ears. And some clinicians, administrators, and support staffers are relatively deaf when it comes to following basic security precautions. To unplug those ears requires more than insisting that they sit through classroom instructions.

It requires addressing a variety of cultural issues and underlying attitudes about security and about healthcare information technology in general. A recent report from the Pell Center for International Relations and Public Policy devoted a section to "Cybersecurity as a People Problem," in which it offers insights on the attitudes that serve as road blocks to a security conscious culture: "Cybersecurity issues often start with ordinary technology users who have not received proper training, do not take security seriously, or prize convenience over security by—consciously or not—sidestepping basic standards of best practices." [3] Add to that list of obstacles several others:

- Physicians' general dissatisfaction for healthcare information technology and dysfunctional electronic health records
- The fact that electronic health records (EHRs) and related security protocols often slow clinicians down and may interfere with patient care
- Reports of medical errors caused by healthcare IT
- The initial loss of productivity and revenue that often results from using EHRs

Many who work in healthcare do not take security very seriously because they are convinced they will not fall victim to the various mistakes or scams that open up holes in an organization's computer network. It is the same mentality that many Americans have about having a screening colonoscopy or giving up tobacco. Colon cancer will affect the other guy. "My father smoked a pack a day and never developed lung cancer."

But the statistics on data breaches clearly demonstrate the risks are greater than the average person imagines. A recent Verizon data breach report found that phishing was involved in one of every 4 data breaches. A Ponemon Institute report says a 10,000 employee company can expect to send $3.7 million a year on phishing attacks [4]. One of the best ways to convince staff members that they are in fact vulnerable is to run a fake phishing scam. They can be quite humbling, even for the most intelligent, tech savvy members of your organization. More details on "white hat" phishing experiments, which test how often employees click on an infected email link, is discussed in more detail in chapter 5: "Reducing the Risk of a Data Breach." Among the vendors who can provide phishing tests to assess your staff's security consciousness are PhishMe, ThreatSim, and KnowBe4.

Addressing the "following security protocols is too inconvenient" mindset requires creating a security policy that clearly spells out the consequences of ignoring those policies, consequences that at the extreme end of the spectrum should include disciplinary action and termination. It is far more inconvenient to lose one's job than to adhere to a few security rules.

Addressing clinicians' dissatisfaction with EHR technology and how it spills over into disregard for related security measures is a far more difficult issue because some of the dissatisfaction is justified. Many EHR systems are poorly designed and do not take into account the normal workflow used in clinical scenarios. Similarly, more than a few physicians continue to complain that all the time spent in front on a computer screen checking boxes is eating into their time caring for patients and reduces the ability to see enough patients per day to keep their practices financially sustainable.

In a survey conducted by AmericanEHR Partners, for instance, physicians voiced complaints like: "It takes twice as long to complete a patient's visit, and I see 75% of the patients now as compared to before EHR," and "The EHR makes every aspect of the work involved with patient care take MUCH longer than it did before." [5] However, research suggests lost productivity may only be temporary. For instance, Hermant Bhargava from the University of California Davis and colleagues found that the productivity of 100 physicians using an EHR system initially dropped by 33% but eventually came back to near pre-installment levels [6].

SEEING THE BIGGER PICTURE

Although there are many legitimate reasons to complain about healthcare IT and security, understanding the history of technology implementation in other industries may persuade clinicians to get on board. In the first part of the 20th century, many manufacturers invested heavily in electricity, replacing water-wheels and steam engines with electric motors to power their equipment. It seemed like a cost effective way to improve productivity but it did not work very well at first because they failed to change essential parts of the antiquated infrastructure used at the time. They continued to use old-fashioned belt-and-pulley systems to transfer the electronic power from the new motors to other parts of their factories. Real productivity gains only occurred after companies reengineered other processes.

The same dynamic holds true in information technology. As Spenser S. Jones, PhD, and his colleagues explain in the *New England Journal of Medicine*:

> "Studies of the IT productivity paradox suggested that the productivity payoff of an IT investment did not follow quickly but instead required periods of intensive process reengineering. For every dollar invested in IT systems, firms typically had to invest several dollars for implementation, training, and process redesign to realize productivity gains. Furthermore, IT-driven productivity growth was not inevitable in all organizations but was more likely in organizations with such characteristics as high levels of education and individual autonomy, self-directed work teams, and incentive systems that reward team performance." [7]

Too many medical practices and hospitals have been content to simply swap out paper filing systems for electronic medical record systems, much like factories that replaced steam engines with electric motors. To see productivity grow, medical practitioners need to give up their "belt-and-pulley" infrastructure, essentially reengineering many of the processes they now use to deliver patient care. In practical terms, that means meeting EHR vendors halfway. EHR vendors need to make a greater effort to design products to accommodate physicians' workflow, but physicians also need to make changes in these workflow processes to accommodate the realities of information technology.

As far as EHRs interfering with patient care, some physicians have learned to make the process of filling out the digital report *part* of the doctor/patient conversation. Since EHRs have been introduced into clinical practice, many patients have complained that they feel ignored because their doctors are spending too much time looking at a computer screen and too little time making eye contact.

There are creative ways to deal with this problem. Sometimes it is as simple as repositioning the computer so that clinicians do not have to turn their backs on patients to make entries. Dan Martich, MD, the chief medical informatics officer at the University of Pittsburgh Medical Center (UPMC), suggests actually making the computer part of the doctor/patient conversation. When he takes a medical history or documents allergies, for instance, he explains to the patient: "UPMC has spent a lot of money on electronic health records. Let me show you how the tool can help me care for you in a more engaged way." [8] Some medical practices and hospitals have also begun hiring scribes, employees whose specific role is to input data into the electronic medical record while the physician carries on a conversation with the patient or performs a physical examination.

Patient safety is another issue that some clinicians bring up among their objections to using EHRs and security protocols. That too is a real issue that should not be trivialized during staff training. The Joint Commission recently issued "Sentinel Event Alert #42" on the safe use of health information technology to address these concerns and to document 120 sentinel events, which the Commission defines as "unexpected occurrences involving death or serious physical or psychological injury, of the risk thereof." The adverse events included a chest x-ray being done on the wrong patient because of an incorrect entry in an EHR and administration of a drug by intramuscular injection rather than the intravenous route because a physician made the wrong choice in a drop down menu.

The Joint Commission alert offers advice on how to reduce the incidence of IT-related events that endanger patients, explained in the reference cited below. But it also states: "On the positive side, however, well-designed and appropriately used EHRs coupled with strong clinical processes can improve and monitor health care quality and safety through their ability to access important medical history data, provide clinical decision support tools, and facilitate communication among providers and between providers and patients. EHRs have demonstrated the ability to reduce adverse events, particularly EHRs with clinical data repository, clinical decision support, computerized provider order entry (CPOE) and provider documentation functionalities." [9]

UNDERSTANDING THE PSYCHOLOGY OF CHANGE

Addressing the aforementioned obstacles is an important part of security education, but so is understanding the psychology of change. Unfortunately, the science in this specialty is rather murky. For decades, psychologists have tried to understand the best way to influence behavior and change entrenched attitudes. At least five prominent theories have been proposed to help decipher the cognitive and emotional issues [10].

Reasoned action. This theory suggests that people make decisions that influence their behavior based on attitudes and social norms—no surprise there. The theory of *planned behavior* contends that a person's attitudes and intentions, subjective norms, and the customary codes of conduct of those around him determine whether he changes his behavior. One researcher [10] explains it this way: "The key component to this model is behavioural intent. Behavioural intentions are influenced by the attitude about the likelihood that the behaviour will have the expected outcome and the subjective evaluation of the risks and benefits of that outcome."

The theory of *protection motivation* postulates that a person makes decisions about changing their behavior in part by doing a threat assessment, taking into account the role of fear in influencing one's health related behaviors.

According to the theory of *self-efficiency*, the decision to adopt a preventive behavior depends on three factors: Whether a person realizes they are at risk, whether they expect the behavior change will reduce that risk, and "the expectation that the person is capable enough to adopt preventive behavior or to refrain from risky health behavior." This perspective is worth considering when commissioning a security education program. More than one expert has pointed out that these sessions often miss their mark because they bombard students with too many things to do and assume they have a grasp of technology beyond what they actually have.

The *expected utility hypothesis*, on the other hand, states that "behavioural change can be explained because individuals perceive it as a 'useful' decision." Usefulness is a relative terms for employees. To be realistic, it is rare to find a staff member who believes an organization's computer network requires as much tender loving care as their home network, which is why it is wise to offer employees attending a security awareness or training session advice that they can apply at home as well as in the office. It is important to put some emphasis on the personal value of the information they are learning.

Educators continue to apply these and other rationales to construct training and awareness programs, but the key question business and physician leaders have to ask is: Do the security education programs actually have a measurable impact. In other words, are they fostering security conscious behavior and fewer security incidents?

Although there is not a great deal of good quality research to answer these questions for the entire American workforce, there are some success stories. Green Clinic, for instance, a medical facility in Ruston, La. has found short monthly notes about specific HIPAA compliance issues to be helpful. So were short tests to assess staffers' retention [4]. Jason Thomas, the CIO and HIPAA security officer at the clinic believes that "It's too easy to overburden people with too many security-centric things at once." Similarly Sailpoint Technologies, on the other hand, uses videos from SANS Institute, including case studies on social engineering scams, to train their staff.

Research on the effectiveness of security education comes from the 2014 US State of Cybercrime Survey by PricewaterhouseCoopers, which said that 42% of respondents found security education and awareness for new employees helped reduce the risk of a potential attack. The same PwC report found companies that did not provide security training for new employees lost about $683,000 a year, while companies with training averaged about $162,000 [11].

Several security specialists believe that training employees to spot a phishing scam before it is too late has a measurable impact. One Fortune 50 company that used fake phishing emails to test their staffers' security skills followed up with a message that made them aware of their mistake if they took the bait. They were sent an immediate training message and also enrolled in a training program to help them avoid such scams in the future. Nearly 35% of employees who received the initial email scam failed the test but in a subsequent test, that number dropped below 6%. The Wombat Security Technologies report that discussed the case pointed out that this approach to security awareness had resulted in an 84% drop in susceptibility [12].

Truly effective staff education must go beyond phishing tests. One of the reasons so many training programs fail to change employees' security awareness is they do not harness all the tricks and techniques that major marketing specialists have been using for decades to sell detergent, toothpaste, and soda. Coca-Cola, for example, has been very successful selling brown sugar water to millions of Americans through the use of brilliant commercials that equate soda with fun times, romance, and family togetherness--despite the fact that a single serving bottle contains the equivalent of 22 packets of sugar, and the overwhelming evidence that the beverage contributes to America's obesity epidemic [13]. If Madison Avenue can pull off that feat, why can't the healthcare industry hire the same spin doctors to promote a worthwhile initiative like security hygiene? Granted, campaigns of this nature are very expensive. But so are multimillion dollar federal fines, class action lawsuits, and all the other expenses that often result from data breaches.

MANAGING THE TRAINING PROCESS

As mentioned earlier, there are many commercial and public resources to help educate your staff on healthcare IT security. The problem with most of these tools is that they rarely include a frank discussion of the barriers and cultural issues mentioned above. With that in mind, you may want to use these resources as a jumping off point, customizing them to include the nagging issues that bother so many clinicians.

But before creating a specific awareness and training program, it is important to consider how the program will be managed. You should have at least one person assigned to manage the program. And that person should establish a timeline for rolling out training sessions, making sure that all new employees receive an initial tutorial as soon as possible. And everyone on staff should be schooled in how to report a privacy or security problem. Also consider quizzing staffers to confirm their grasp of the materials. Lastly, do not make the mistake of thinking security and privacy training is a one-time event. It needs to be ongoing, with follow-up training as changes in your organization's policies and procedures unfold.

WHAT SHOULD THE TRAINING CONSIST OF?

Depending on the size of your organization, your budget, and your organization's business objectives, you may decide to use pre-designed training materials or build them from the ground up, hiring an educational specialist to create a customized program.

What exactly should security training include? In addition to providing an overview of the HIPAA Privacy and Security Rules and what they are designed to accomplish, training should cover many of the basic security safeguards discussed in the previous chapters: Creating strong passwords, not clicking on suspicious links in emails, locking down mobile devices when possible, not using file sharing programs, safe web browsing to name a few. Also keep in mind that different members of the healthcare team will need different types of information, depending on their responsibilities.

A detailed course outline is beyond the scope of the book, but Rebecca Herold and Kevin Beaver's textbook on HIPAA privacy and security compliance provides an entire chapter on how to design training and awareness programs [14]. Herold and Beaver explore the various groups that need to be educated and the varied needs, what specialized topics should be covered for specific groups, how to design the modules, the differences between awareness and training programs, and how to measure the effectiveness of these programs.

If, on the other hand, you want to take a simpler, less costly approach, there are numerous outlines and PowerPoint presentations available. The University of North Carolina at Chapel Hill has a HIPAA, Privacy and Security Training Module available—for non-commercial use [15]. The US Department of Health and Human Services' Office of Civil Rights, in conjunction with Medscape, has prepared a CME program entitled "Patient Privacy: A Guide for Providers." [16] KnowBe4 offers free and paid security training resources at www.knowbe4.com.

HHS also has its own "Information Systems Security Awareness Training" slide show that offers an overview of information security, and discusses physical access controls, email and Internet security, security outside the office, privacy, and incident reporting [17]. The slide show takes about an hour to work through and contains test questions throughout. Since the presentation was originally designed for government employees, it contains a form at the end in which the student signs off, acknowledging they took the course and agreeing to follow its guidelines.

One of the most important components of any staff training program should be a tutorial on phishing. Considering how many major data breaches have resulted from employees being fooled by hackers posing as friends, colleagues, bosses, or threatening officials, there is no way to *overemphasize* the need to educate healthcare staff on their tricks. Knowbe4 has an excellent graphic that illustrates several of the mistakes email users make when exposed to phishing scams. As Fig. 8.1 shows, email users have to scrutinize every component of their emails to look for clues. That includes the From line, the To line, the Date, the Subject, and the link in the body of the text. Granted, this kind of scrutiny will initially slow down employees' productivity, but once it becomes second nature, things will speed up again.

Among the questions the email recipient needs to ask herself:

- Is the sender's email address from a suspicious domain?
- Is it an unusual email with a link or an attachment from a person I do not usually communicate with?
- Are there misspellings in the email?
- Is the message a reply to something I never asked for?
- Is the message from someone or organization that I do have dealings with but the email address is slightly different from the correct address—even by one character?
- When you place your cursor over the link in the email main text, is the address different than what it says in the link?

As I have mentioned before, there is no such thing as an impenetrable fortress. And the US Department of Health and Human Services realizes that. It does not penalize healthcare organizations for every single HIPAA violation or data

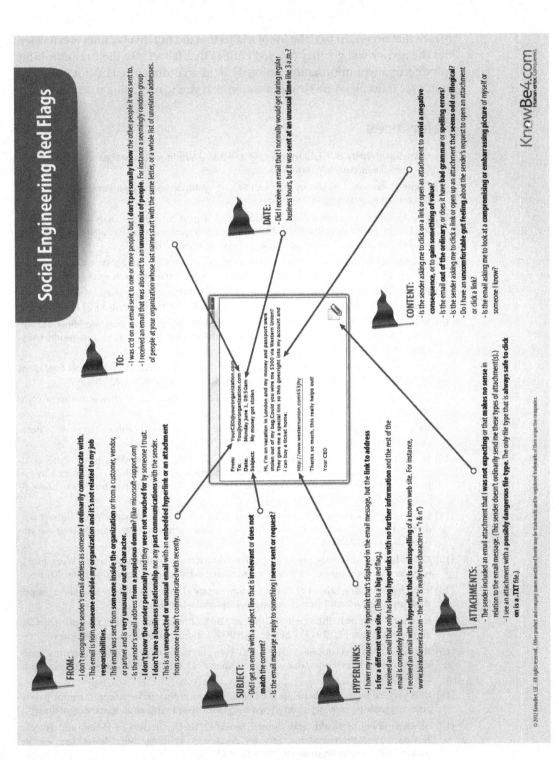

FIGURE 8.1 Red flags that suggest an email is a phishing scam.

Source: Courtesy of KnowBe4, Clearwater, FL.

breach that occurs. In fact, the list of snafus that did not involve fines is extensive. But the agency will go after covered entities that fail to take their responsibility to protect patient information seriously. And according to HHS, not providing employee training is one clear indication that you're not taking it seriously.

References

[1] Cornell University Law Library. 45 CFR 164.308—Administrative safeguards. https://www.law.cornell.edu/cfr/text/45/164.308.

[2] Cornell University Law Library. 45 CFR 164.530—Administrative requirements. https://www.law.cornell.edu/cfr/text/45/164.530.

[3] K.S. Spidalieri. Professionalizing cybersecurity: a path to universal standards and status, PELL CENTER for INTERNATIONAL RELATIONS. https://www.salve.edu/sites/default/files/filesfield/documents/Professionalizing-Cybersecurity.pdf, 2014.

[4] M. Korolov. Does security awareness training even work? CSO. http://www.csoonline.com/article/2987822/data-protection/does-security-awareness-training-even-work.html, 2015.

[5] P. Cerrato. How to ease EHR frustration, InformationWeek. http://www.informationweek.com/healthcare/electronic-health-records/how-to-ease-ehr-frustration/d/d-id/1104207,2012.

[6] M.S. Merrill. Study: EMRs' effect on docs' productivity depends on needs, workflow, Healthcare IT News. http://www.healthcareitnews.com/news/study-emrs-effect-docs-productivity-depends-needs-workflow, 2010.

[7] S.S. Jones, et al. Unraveling the IT productivity paradox—lessons for health care. N Engl J Med 366 (2012) 2243–2245. http://www.nejm.org/doi/full/10.1056/NEJMp1204980.

[8] P. Cerrato. Do your EHR manners turn patients off? Medscape. http://www.medscape.com/viewarticle/809237, 2013.

[9] The Joint Commission. Sentinel even alert, Issue 54, Safe use of health information technology. http://www.jointcommission.org/assets/1/18/SEA_54.pdf, 2015.

[10] M. Bada, A. Sasse. Global cyber security capacity centre: draft working paper: cyber security awareness campaigns why do they fail to change behaviour? Global Cyber Security Capacity Centre. https://www.sbs.ox.ac.uk/cybersecurity-capacity/system/files/Awareness%20CampaignsDraftWorkingPaper.pdf, 2014.

[11] F.Y. Rashid. Is security awareness training really worth it? InformationWeek http://www.darkreading.com/operations/careers-and-people/is-security-awareness-training-really-worth-it/d/d-id/1317573, 2014.

[12] F.Y. Rashid. Security awareness training debate: does it make a difference? Security Week. http://www.securityweek.com/security-awareness-training-debate-does-it-make-difference, 2013.

[13] T.H. Harvard. Chan School of Public Health. Sugary Drinks and Obesity Fact Sheet. http://www.hsph.harvard.edu/nutritionsource/sugary-drinks-fact-sheet/.

[14] R. Herold, K. Beaver, The Practical Guide to HIPAA Privacy and Security Compliance, CRC Press, Boca Raton, FL, (2015) Chapter 25 HIPAA Training, Education, and Awareness.

[15] University of North Carolina at Chapel Hill. Welcome to the HIPAA, Privacy & Security Training Module. https://www.unc.edu/hipaa/Annual%20HIPAA%20Training%20current.pdf, 2013–2015.

[16] HHS.gov. Training materials: helping entities implement privacy and security protections, patient privacy: a guide for providers. http://www.hhs.gov/ocr/privacy/hipaa/understanding/training/.

[17] US Department of Health and Human Services. The Department of Health and Human Services Information Systems Security Awareness Training. http://www.hhs.gov/ocio/securityprivacy/awarenesstraining/issa.pdf, 2015.

CHAPTER 9

HIPAA, HITECH, and the Business Associate

Whether you manage a healthcare provider organization or run a company that works with one or more of these organizations, you need to concern yourself with HIPAA regulations and other laws governing the use of protected health information (PHI). As I mentioned in chapter 3: Regulations Governing Protected Health Information, for the purposes of HIPAA, a business associate is: "A person or entity who, on behalf of a covered entity, performs or assists in performance of a function or activity involving the use or disclosure of individually identifiable health information, such as data analysis, claims processing or administration, utilization review, and quality assurance reviews... Business associates are also persons or entities performing legal, actuarial, accounting, consulting, data aggregation, management, administrative, accreditation, or financial services to or for a covered entity where performing those services involves disclosure of individually identifiable health information by the covered entity or another business associate of the covered entity to that person or entity." [1]

If on the other hand, a vendor is handling de-identified patient data—that is, information that cannot be traced back to an individual patient—it is not officially a BA in the HIPAA sense of the term. Similarly, if a vendor does not come in contact with PHI, the regulations do not apply.

The regulations governing BAs have changed over the years. In the original HIPAA regulations, first enacted in 1996, BAs were not considered liable if a data breach that exposed PHI occurred as a result of their lax security measures. The Omnibus Final Rule of 2013, ushered in with the Health Information Technology for Economic and Clinical Health Act (HITECH), changed all that. BAs now share the responsibilities with "covered entities," including hospitals and other healthcare organizations, to keep patient data secure.

Regulations 45 CFR.164.402(c), 164.504(e), 164.532(d) and (e) state that a vendor is required to provide reasonable assurances that it will use sensitive patient information only for the purposes for which the company was engaged by the healthcare organization. It also must show evidence that it will safeguard that information from misuse and will help the healthcare organization comply with some of the organization's duties under the HIPAA Privacy Rule.

The rules also point out that the covered entity can only disclose PHI to a BA so that the BA can help the healthcare organization carry out its function in providing health services. That means vendors are forbidden from using this sensitive information for any independent purposes. Outside of the healthcare world, vendors often "double-dip" when collecting data, using it not just to process a customer order for merchandise, for instance, but adding their personal information to a database that has value in their marketing efforts or as part of a for-rent mailing list. HIPAA makes it clear: no double-dipping.

EVALUATING THE THREAT

A search of the US Department of Health and Human Services' Office of Civil Rights (OCR) database of data breaches affecting 500 or more individuals revealed that as of November 2015, business associates were involved in at least 62 breaches. However, according to a 2014 analysis of the same OCR "Wall of Shame" data reported in *Becker's Health IT and CIO Review,* BAs were responsible for 58% of patient records breached [2]. Among the businesses that reported breaches, according to the report, were Iron Mountain, Towers Watson, McKesson, ADP, and K-Mart.

The *Fifth Annual Benchmark Study on Privacy & Security of Healthcare Data,* published in May 2015 by the well-respected Ponemon Institute, agreed with *Becker's* assessment. It found that "59 percent of business associates had at least one data breach involving the loss or theft of patient data in the past 24 months. In fact, 29 percent say their organization had more than 2 breaches." [3] (The study included 88 BAs.) Seven out of 10 BAs who responded to the Ponemon survey said they have experienced between 11 and 30 events that were described as "electronic information-based security incidents." Most involved fewer than 100 PHI records. The same report found that the average cost of a data breach for a BA topped $1 million. Thirty nine percent of these data breaches were caused by a criminal attacker and ten percent by an insider. Despite these disturbed statistics, only 35% of BAs say they are concerned about cyber attackers.

When you analyze the resources that BAs have at their disposal to build an adequate security platform that would prevent or at least reduce the risk of a data breach, it becomes clear that incidents are not going away any time soon. The Ponemon report found that more than half (59%) of BAs do not think their incident response process has enough funding or resources. Adding insult to injury, more than half of BAs, as well as health care organizations, "fail to perform a risk assessment for security incidents, despite the federal mandate to do so."

Additional statistics that provide some insight into the state of security among the many vendors, consultants, and organizations that serve as BAs to the healthcare industry include the following:

- Only 50% of BA personnel have the technical expertise to spot and resolve data breaches
- 50% of BAs have adequate policies and procedures in place to prevent or detect unauthorized data access, data losses, or theft
- 46% of BAs have technologies in place to prevent or detect these incidents quickly

As important as it is to be prepared for the possibility of a data breach before one occurs, it is also necessary to handle these incidents after they occur. Common sense dictates the need for an adequate breach response. Unfortunately, that point of view has not taken hold among many businesses working with the healthcare industry. The aforementioned report found that only 6% of BAs who had some sort of security incident that involved electronic documents hired outside legal help, an auditing firm, or other third party to help assessment the future risk. Only 10% used a third party automated process or software tool to assess their risk. In fact, only 13% even have a formal approach to incident response management.

Like the healthcare organizations they serve, BAs share many of the same security snafus. Among the security incidents that they have experienced, those caused by lost or stolen devices top the list (95%), followed by spear phishing scams (90%). They were followed in descending order by web-borne malware attacks, and advanced persistent threats or targeted attacks.

Although many of the data breaches affecting the healthcare industry find their way onto the OCR list of data breaches, not all the security incidents involving businesses do for a variety of reasons, including the fact that breaches affecting fewer than 500 individuals are not listed on the OCR site, and the fact that OCR does not typically deal with data breaches in which businesses have direct contact with consumers. A report from the Federal Trade Commission is more revealing in that respect. A 2014 FTC privacy and data security update also provides some insights on the types of data breaches these businesses cause [4]. Among the settlements are the following:

> An Atlanta-based health billing company and its former CEO settled FTC charges that they misled thousands of consumers who signed up for an online billing portal by failing to adequately inform them that the company would seek highly detailed medical information from pharmacies, medical labs, and insurance companies. Payments MD, LLC, and its former CEO, Michael C. Hughes, allegedly used the sign-up process for a "Patient Portal'—where consumers could view their billing history—as a pathway to

deceptively seek consumers' consent to obtain detailed medical information about the consumers.

In its 50th data security settlement, the FTC settled allegations that GMR Transcription Services—an audio file transcription service—violated the FTC Act. According to the complaint, GMR relied on service providers and independent typists to transcribe files for their clients, which include healthcare providers. As a result of GMR's alleged failure to implement reasonable security measures and oversee its service providers, at least 15,000 files containing sensitive personal information—including consumers' names, birthdates, and medical histories—were available to anyone on the Internet.

ARE YOU A BUSINESS ASSOCIATE?

If you work with a hospital, medical practice, health plan, or healthcare clearinghouse, you may fall under the umbrella that the federal government defines as a BA. If, for example, your company assists a health insurance company with claims processing, you are a HIPAA responsible BA. If you are a certified public accountant that provides services to a hospital or medical practice and have access to PHI, you too are accountable.

Others who fall into this category include attorneys who offer services to a health plan, hospital, clinic, or physician office, if they have access to patient information; a consultant that does utilization review for a hospital, a healthcare clearing house that converts claims from a nonstandard format into a standard transaction on behalf of a healthcare provider and forwards the processed transaction to a payer. And since HIPAA healthcare clearinghouses can also be covered entities, this means an organization can fall into both categories.

Similarly, a transcriptionist that transcribes physicians' notes is also considered a BA, assuming he or she is an independent vendor. Someone who works as an employee for the medical practice is not a BA. A Pharmacy benefits manager that manages a health plan's pharmacist network is defined as a BA by HHS [5]. Others that will likely be considered BAs include answering services, patient safety organizations, IT and security consultants, and subcontractors of BAs [6]. To quote the HHS OCR, "A 'business associate' also is a subcontractor that creates, receives, maintains, or transmits protected health information on behalf of another business associate." [6]

Additional business functions that would qualify a company as a BA include data analytics, practice management, repricing, data aggregation, data de-identification services, actuarial services, administrative services, accreditation groups, and financial firms. Once again, being classified as a BA depends on the nature of the relationship of the business to the healthcare organization and its exposure to PHI. There will be gray areas in which there is no clear-cut way to determine whether a sole proprietor or company is a BA as outlined in the HIPAA regulations, which it why it is wise to consult an attorney with expertise in healthcare to assist in making that determination. Among the agents that are sometimes considered BAs: internet service providers, software vendors, and companies that provide personal health record systems on behalf of a covered entity.

Let's take software vendors as an example. The fact that a company sells or provides software to a hospital or medical practice in itself does not establish a BA relationship if the vendor does not have access to PHI from that covered entity. But if it needs to have access to patient data in order to provide its service to the healthcare organization, it would then be categorized as a BA. And even if the vendor's service does not require routine access to that data, it may still be considered a BA if it has to troubleshoot the software and is exposed to PHI in that context. One exception to that rule is when an employee of a contractor, like a software or information technology vendor, has his or her primary duty station on-site at a covered entity. In that case, the covered entity may choose to treat the employee of the vendor as a member of the covered entity's workforce, rather than as a business associate.

HIPAA and HITECH primarily concern themselves with the privacy and security of patient data in the hands of healthcare organizations and the businesses they deal with. A vendor that offers a personal health records service directly to the public rather than on behalf of a hospital, medical practice, or health insurer, on the other hand, is *not* a BA according to HIPAA regulations because HIPAA does not govern this component of healthcare. The Federal Trade Commission is responsible for monitoring businesses that offer direct health related services to the public, including personal health record programs. But if you are a business associate that only handles PHI for a HIPAA covered entity, like a hospital, medical practice, or insurance plan, the FTC rules on data breaches and securing patient data do not apply to your business.

FTC explains its jurisdiction this way:

> Does your business or organization have a website that allows people to maintain their medical information online? Do you provide applications for personal health records – say, a device that allows people to upload readings from a blood pressure cuff or pedometer into their personal health record? The American Recovery and Reinvestment Act of 2009 includes provisions to strengthen privacy and security protections for this new sector of web-based businesses. The law directed the Federal Trade Commission to issue a rule requiring companies to contact customers in the event of a security breach.

The FTC issued the Health Breach Notification Rule to cover this situation, and the rule is very similar to the one that applies to BAs who violate the HIPAA regulations, namely the company is required to notify everyone whose information was breached, notify the FTC, and in many cases, notify the media [7]. Needless to say, that last requirement has the potential to destroy a health related business that relies on public trust.

FORMAL AGREEMENTS ARE A MUST

The Office for Civil Rights has a web page on which it lists case examples of mistakes and violations made by healthcare providers and business associates. In one scenario, it explains:

> A complaint alleged that a law firm working on behalf of a pharmacy chain in an administrative proceeding impermissibly disclosed the PHI of a customer of the pharmacy chain. OCR investigated the allegation and found no evidence that the law firm had impermissibly disclosed the customer's PHI. However, the investigation revealed that the pharmacy chain and the law firm had not entered into a Business Associate Agreement, as required by the Privacy Rule to ensure that PHI is appropriately safeguarded. Without a properly executed agreement, a covered entity may not disclose PHI to its law firm. To resolve the matter, OCR required the pharmacy chain and the law firm to enter into a business associate agreement [8].

Regulation 45 CFR 164.504(e) clearly states the need for a contract or some other form of written agreement [9] between healthcare organizations and business associates. (Healthcare organizations and BAs are expected to have contracts in place that reflect the regulations spelled out in the Omnibus Final Rule as of Sept 22, 2014.) Three of the most important items that must be included in the agreement are the following:

- Describe the permitted and required uses of protected health information by the BA
- State that the BA will not use or further disclose the protected health information other than as permitted or required by the contract or as required by law
- Require the BA use appropriate safeguards to prevent a use or disclosure of the protected health information other than as provided for by the contract

If the BA compromises patient data or otherwise commits a HIPAA violation and the healthcare organization becomes aware of it, it is obligated to take reasonable steps to cure the breach or end the violation. If such steps are unsuccessful, it is obligated to terminate the contract or arrangement. If termination of the contract or agreement is not feasible, the organization is required to report the problem to the Office for Civil Rights.

If you manage a business or are an individual working with a hospital, medical practice or other covered entity, keep in mind that there are some exceptions to the BA standard. In these situations, the healthcare organization does *not* need to have a written agreement in place before it shares patient information. For example, if a hospital sends a patient to a specialist for treatment, there is no need for a BA agreement. The two can send patient information back and forth for the purposes of treating the patient. Of course, the specialist still needs to take reasonable precautions to keep the data safe.

Similarly, if a physician wants to send PHI to a lab to assist in the patient's treatment, there is no need for a BA agreement. And a hospital laboratory is not required to have a business associate contract to disclose protected health information to a reference laboratory for treatment of the individual. The common denominator in all these transactions is the fact that a patient's *treatment* is directly involved. That said, there are circumstances in which even a healthcare provider would be considered a BA to another healthcare provider. For example, a hospital may enlist the services of another health care provider to assist in the hospital's training of medical students. In this case, a business associate contract would be required before the hospital could allow the health care provider access to patient health information.

There are several other situations in which a BA contract or other written agreement is not needed. If you are running a group insurance plan, it is not necessary to have such an agreement in order to share PHI with the plan's sponsor—an employer for instance. One caveat, however, to keep in mind according to OCR is that the group health plan's documents have been amended to limit the disclosures.

Another exception outlined by OCR involves "the collection and sharing of protected health information by a health plan that is a public benefits program, such as Medicare, and an agency other than the agency administering the health plan, such as the Social Security Administration, that collects protected health information to determine eligibility or enrollment, or determines eligibility or enrollment, for the government program, where the joint activities are authorized by law."

MORE EXCEPTIONS TO THE RULE

There are so many unique situations in healthcare, and that variety explains where there are so many exceptions to the HIPAA requirement that BAs and healthcare organizations have a written agreement when sharing PHI.

Let's say you are a physician or nurse practitioner submitting a claim for reimbursement after treating a patient. Typically it is necessary to share details of the patient's diagnosis and treatment plan with the insurance company to qualify for reimbursement. That disclosure of PHI on the part of the clinician does not require a BA agreement on the part of the insurance company. In this scenario, both the clinician and the insurer are considered covered entities, not business associates.

If your hospital or clinic hires a janitorial service or plumber, it is unlikely they will have access to patient information, in which case there is no need for a BA contract. In fact, OCR goes a bit further, stating there would be no need for a written agreement even if these persons or companies had "incidental" access to PHI. There are other similar situations in which an independent agent would not need a BA agreement. For example, the US Postal Service, certain private couriers, and electronic "couriers" do not need them because they are simply serving as conduits of the patient data.

Another special situation applies to organized health care arrangements (OHCAs). If for instance, a group health plan buys insurance from a health insurance issuer or HMO, the relationship between the group health plan and the health insurance issuer or HMO is defined by the Privacy Rule as an OHCA, with respect to the individuals they jointly serve. Under circumstances like this, these two entities are considered covered entities and are therefore permitted to share protected health information that relates to the joint health care activities of the OHCA.

Another example: If one covered entity purchases a health plan product or other insurance, for example, reinsurance, from an insurer. Each entity is acting on its own behalf when the covered entity purchases the insurance benefits, and when the covered entity submits a claim to the insurer and the insurer pays the claim.

Hospitals, medical practices and other healthcare organizations and professionals are also allowed to reveal protected health information to a researcher for research purposes, either with patient authorization, which would involve a waiver under 45 CFR 164.512(i), or as a limited data set as spelled out in 45 CFR 164.514(e). Because the researcher is not conducting a function or activity regulated by the Administrative Simplification Rules, such as payment or health care operations, or providing one of the services listed in the definition of a BA in the HIPAA regulations, the researcher is not a business associate of the covered entity, and no business associate agreement is required.

If a financial institution processes consumer-conducted financial transactions by debit, credit, or other payment card, clears checks, initiates or processes electronic funds transfers, or conducts any other activity that directly facilitates or effects the transfer of funds for payment for health care or health plan premiums, no BA agreement is warranted. When it conducts these activities, the financial institution is providing its normal banking or other financial transaction services to its customers; it is not performing a function or activity for, or on behalf of, the covered entity.

Since institutional review boards are involved in reviewing research and having oversight of research projects, they are also not considered BAs [6].

WHAT SHOULD A BUSINESS ASSOCIATE AGREEMENT LOOK LIKE?

The regulations governing BAs make it clear that they are *directly* liable under the HIPAA/HITECH rules and subject to civil and in some cases criminal penalties for using and disclosing PHI in a way that is not authorized by the written agreements they sign with healthcare organizations. It is important to realize, however, that BAs are liable for HIPAA violations even if they do not have an agreement in place with a healthcare organization [10].

Earlier in this chapter, I mentioned three of the most important items that need to be included in a BA agreement. There are more. The agreement should stipulate that:

- The business associate will report to the covered entity any use or disclosure of the information not provided for by its contract, including incidents that constitute breaches of unsecured protected health information.
- As you may recall, under HIPAA, a healthcare provider has an obligation to make patient records available to the patients themselves. BAs have a similar obligation and the agreement should make it clear that the BA will disclose protected health information as specified in its contract to satisfy a hospital's or medical practice's obligation with respect to individuals' requests for copies of their protected health information, as well as make available protected health information for amendments (and incorporate any amendments, if required) and accountings.
- To the extent the business associate is to carry out a covered entity's obligation under the Privacy Rule, the agreement will require the business associate to comply with the requirements applicable to the obligation and require the business associate to make available to HHS its internal practices, books, and records relating to the use and disclosure of protected health information received from, or created or received by the business associate on behalf of, the covered entity for purposes of HHS determining the covered entity's compliance with the HIPAA Privacy Rule.

- When the contract between the healthcare provider and BA is terminated, the agreement should state that the BA has to return or destroy all protected health information that it received from the provider, and any PHI that was created by the business associate, if that is feasible.
- The agreement should also require the business associate to ensure that any subcontractors it may engage on its behalf that will have access to protected health information agree to the same restrictions and conditions that apply to the business associate with respect to such information.
- Finally the agreement should authorize termination of the contract by the covered entity if the BA violates one of the terms of the contract. Contracts between business associates and business associates that are subcontractors are subject to these same requirements.

In the appendix on page 133, you will find a sample BA agreement from OCR, Keep in mind that the words in brackets are intended as either optional language or as instructions to the users of these sample provisions. Several other organizations have drafted similar sample agreements, including the University of Texas Health Science Center in San Antonio [11] and the Fox Group, LLC [12].

References

[1] Department of Health and Human Services National Institutes of Health. To whom does the privacy rule apply and whom will it affect? http://privacyruleandresearch.nih.gov/pr_06.asp.

[2] M.A. Chaput. Business associates: a greater security threat than hackers, Becker's Health IT & CIO Review. http://www.beckershospitalreview.com/healthcare-information-technology/business-associates-a-greater-security-threat-than-hackers.html, 2014.

[3] Ponemon Institute. Fifth Annual Benchmark Study on Privacy, ID Experts. https://www2.idexpertscorp.com/fifth-annual-ponemon-study-on-privacy-security-incidents-of-healthcare-data, 2015.

[4] FTC 1 Federal Trade Commission 2014 Privacy and Data Security Update. https://www.ftc.gov/system/files/documents/reports/privacy-data-security-update-2014/privacydatasecurityupdate_2014.pdf.

[5] Department of Health and Human Services. Business associates. http://www.hhs.gov/ocr/privacy/hipaa/understanding/coveredentities/businessassociates.html.

[6] R. Herold, K. Beaver, The Practical Guide to HIPAA Privacy and Security Compliance, second ed., CRC Press, New York, 2015, p. 317.

[7] Federal Trade Commission. Health Breach Notification Rule. https://www.ftc.gov/tips-advice/business-center/guidance/health-breach-notification-rule.

[8] HHS.gov. Office for Civil Rights. All case examples: pharmacy chain enters into business associate agreement with law firm. http://www.hhs.gov/ocr/privacy/hipaa/enforcement/examples/allcases.html#case20.

[9] HHS.gov. Office of Civil Rights. Business associate contracts, Sample business associate agreement provisions. http://www.hhs.gov/ocr/privacy/hipaa/understanding/coveredentities/contractprov.html.

[10] *WEDI* McClure JR Gordon-Nguyen M. Business Associates, HITECH & the Omnibus HIPAA Final Rule. US Office of Health and Human Services Office of Civil Rights Webinar presentation. http://www.wedi.org/forms/uploadFiles/35FE700000100.filename.7.26_Combined.pdf.

[11] UT Health Science Center, San Antonio. Sample business associate agreement provisions. http://uthscsa.edu/hipaa/assoc-contract.asp.

[12] Fox Group LLC. Free business associate agreement template. http://www.foxgrp.com/landing-pages/free-business-associate-agreement-template/.

CHAPTER 10

Preparing for and Coping With a Data Breach

The book's title promised a discussion of risk, prevention, and damage control. Chapter 3: Regulations Governing Protected Health Information discussed risk assessment and chapter 5: Reducing the Risk of a Data Breach went into detail on preventing a data breach, or at least mitigating the odds of one happening. This chapter will focus on the damage control part of the equation.

Some security specialists believe that healthcare data breaches are inevitable, but that kind of thinking can encourage complacency on the part of managers, administrators, and clinicians. The likelihood of a security incident or a full scale data breach can be significantly reduced when decision makers insist on the strongest preventive measures, as discussed in chapter 5: Reducing the Risk of a Data Breach. Nonetheless healthcare organizations have to work under the assumption that they will someday be compromised and use a 2-pronged approach to the problem. Make sure a data-breach response plan is in place *long before* any breach occurs. And understand all the steps your organization needs to take if a breach does occur. Experian, the large credit reporting agency, sums up the matter in its *Data Breach Response Guide* "After a data breach has been discovered is not the time to decide how you're going to respond or who will be responsible for addressing the many challenges it poses. It's critical to develop your response plan and build your response team well before you need them." [1]

HOW BAD IS THE SITUATION?

A recent report in *HealthData Management* pointed out that in 2015, there were 109,671,626 Americans affected in 10 major healthcare cyberattacks that occurred [2]. Among the worst attacks listed in their tally:

- *Anthem*: 78.8 million
- *Premera BlueCross*: 11 million
- *Excellus BlueCross BlueShield*: 10 million
- *UCL Health*: 4.5 million
- *Medical Informatics Engineering*: 3.9 million

- *CareFirst BlueCross BlueShield*: 1.1 million
- *Beacon Health System in Indiana*: 220,000
- *Advantage Dental*: 151,626

PREPARING FOR THE WORST

In chapter 4: Risk Assessment, I spoke about the long list of HIPAA regulations provided in the Code of Federal Regulations (CFR). CFR 164.308(a)(6) contains two relevant regulations that cover preparing for and managing security incidents and data breaches:

"(i) Standard: Security incident procedures. Implement policies and procedures to address security incidents.

(ii) Implementation specification: Response and reporting (Required). Identify and respond to suspected or known security incidents; mitigate, to the extent practicable, harmful effects of security incidents that are known to the covered entity or business associate; and document security incidents and their outcomes." [3]

Having policies and procedures in place to cope with security incidents makes little sense if your organization does not have a response team in place to utilize those policies and procedures. Communication and privacy are two of the most important issues that arise during a security incident and these issues are best handled by a well-coordinated team. Even in a small to medium size medical practice, it is easy to mishandle an incident if the lines of communication among physician leaders, IT consultants, staff clinicians, and lawyers involved in the incident are not clearly established. In larger organizations, it can be even more challenging as the chief information officer, human resource director, compliance officer, and risk management director enter the picture. Privacy is equally important. Anyone directly or indirectly involved in handling the incident must be given notice that they cannot discuss any details with others in the organization unless absolutely necessary.

Besides communication and privacy, documentation is also key during any security incident or breach of protected health information (PHI). Among the list of forms and resources recommended by Herzig and associates in their HIMSS guide to information security: [4]

- Incident report form
- Risk assessment to outline what data has been leaked
- A template for a breach notification letter
- A plan of action on how to handle incoming phone calls from patients and employees whose information has been exposed
- An agreement with a credit monitoring service

Once again, it is best to have these resources in place before a breach occurs.

MANAGING SECURITY INCIDENTS AND DATA BREACHES

To reiterate the differences between a security incident, HIPAA violation, and a breach that exposes PHI: A security/privacy incident usually refers to some action or event that does not comply with your organization's policies and procedures, whereas a violation usually refers to an incident that is not compliant with government regulations. Finally a breach refers to a violation that exposes PHI.

The Health Insurance Portability and Accountability Act of 1996 (HIPAA) was updated in 2013 with the final Omnibus Rule, which strengthened patients' privacy protection and the security measures required to keep their records safe. These new regulations are based on statutory changes under the HITECH Act. That final rule is outlined in the Federal Register of January 25, 2013 [5].

The US Department of Health and Human Services says "A breach is, generally, an impermissible use or disclosure under the Privacy Rule that compromises the security or privacy of the protected health information. An impermissible use or disclosure of protected health information is *presumed to be a breach unless the covered entity or business associate, as applicable, demonstrates that there is a low probability that the protected health information has been compromised* based on a risk assessment of at least the following factors: [6]

1. The nature and extent of the protected health information involved, including the types of identifiers and the likelihood of re-identification;
2. The unauthorized person who used the protected health information or to whom the disclosure was made;
3. Whether the protected health information was actually acquired or viewed; and
4. The extent to which the risk to the protected health information has been mitigated."

I have added the italics to the previous text to emphasize that this is a significant change from the older rule, which stated that unsecured PHI was considered a HIPAA violation if it posed a significant risk of financial, reputational, or other harm to the individual. Healthcare organizations no longer have that "loophole." It is assumed that a data breach is a HIPAA violation unless they can show it is unlikely the unsecured data was compromised. A detailed analysis of the difference between the old and new rule is beyond the scope of this book and keeps healthcare attorneys busy splitting hairs. But suffice it to say: The rule is stricter than it used to be and requires more diligence on the part of decision makers and their direct reports.

If a data breach occurs, the notifications required will vary depending in part on how many individuals were affected. OCR has two online procedures for notification, one for breaches affecting 500 or more persons and one for fewer than 500 persons. In the former case, you have to notify the Secretary of HHS "without unreasonable delay and in no case later than 60 calendar days from the discovery of the breach." If on the other hand, fewer than 500 are affected, you are allowed to notify HHS within 60 days of the end of the calendar year in which the breach was discovered. But the government emphasizes that you are not *required* to wait that long. And given all the consequences of a data breach, sooner is usually better. The longer affected patients and employees have to wait to find out their medical and/or personal identity has been compromised, the more likely that information will be sold on the black market, and the less happy they will be about your management of the breach. Unfortunately, that discontent has a way of turning into class action lawsuits and a damaged reputation in the community that you serve.

CREATING A COMPREHENSIVE RESPONSE PLAN

The complexities and financial repercussions of a data breach are so far reaching that anything short of a detailed, expertly conceived plan of action will likely fail. In addition to enlisting the services of an attorney, IT professionals, forensic specialists, public relations experts, and others, you may also want to consider bringing in a specialty group that can manage the entire process, sometimes referred to as a "breach resolution partner." These companies can coordinate all the interacting parts of the process and lift the burden from the shoulders of senior management.

Of course, hiring these partners will depend on the size of your organization and your budget, but they are certainly worth considering. The three credit agencies—Experian [7], TransUnion [8], and Equifax [9]—each offers these services. Since these agencies already have a great deal of experience managing identity theft, they can also offer specific services in addition to managing the overall breach response, including credit monitoring, identity restoration programs, and identity-theft insurance.

But even if you choose not to bring in a breach resolution partner, you can still benefit from the informational resources they provide. The *Data Breach Response Guide* published by Experian, for instance, outlines a well-organized approach that is worth a closer look. It recommends a 10-step approach that starts with (1) the discovery of the breach, (2) investigation and remediation, (3) assembly of an internal response team, (4) reaching out to law enforcement agencies depending on the nature of the breach, (5) bringing in external experts, including the aforementioned breach resolution partner, a forensics team, public relations companies, and lawyers, (6) notification of all necessary persons and regulatory agencies, including federal and state authorities, (7) making a public announcement and creating a website where affected individuals can get assistance, (8) notifying those who have been affected through mail and email, (9), setting up a response mechanism that allows your organization to field questions and complaints, for example, a call center, and (10) getting back to normal business operations while arming yourself for another possible breach.

One of the most useful lists provided in the Experian guide concerns what to do in the first 24 h after the breach is discovered. And whether your organization is a small medical practice or a large academic medical center, these steps all make sense—and may be overlooked in the panic of the moment. The checklist includes common sense things such as recording the date and time the breach was discovered; securing the area around where the breach occurred to preserve any physical or digital evidence; taking infected computers off line, if possible, or finding other ways to stop the leak; interviewing anyone who discovered the leak; documenting the investigation; and bringing in a forensics team to do an in-depth analysis.

The last check box on forensics is worth additional discussion. I have worked with countless physicians—including several world-class scientists—for over 30 years, as a medical editor, educational consultant, and technical writer. During that time, I have discovered that a small percentage of these health professionals suffer from a disease called "genius-itis." Their high IQ, exceptional clinical skills, self-assuredness, and professional success have convinced them that they can solve virtually any problem that comes their way. Occasionally you hear of such gifted individuals even claiming they can defend themselves in medical malpractice suits or can take on other Holmesian feats that mere mortals might shrink from. That kind of hubris has no place during a data breach. Physician leaders and other healthcare decision makers need all the humility they can muster in order to accept the fact they need expert help, especially when it involves performing a forensic root cause analysis of the data breach.

When a breach occurs that exposes PHI, HHS/OCR will be doing an investigation of its own to understand how much culpability rests at your feet. Without a detailed explanation of how the breach occurred and who was at fault, your organization may not be able to avoid a large fine. You need a chain of evidence to establish exactly how and why your facility leaked sensitive patient information, and collecting that evidence often exceeds the expertise of IT consultants who do not specialize in forensic analysis. Winston Krone, managing director at Kivu Consulting, an investigative and analysis service company, points out that regulators are not inclined to accept your explanation of what happened during a breach without evidence. "I think it's fair to say, it sort of raises an eyebrow about those organizations that aren't using forensic analysis or simply trusting whatever a third party has told them about what happened... If you don't do forensics, you're opening yourself up to be destroyed in court. It's a given, and it's expected." [10]

There are several other reasons to perform a forensic analysis. If the data breach involved more than 500 individuals, you are required by law to notify not just HHS and the persons who have had their records compromised. You are also obligated to notify the media. And once the press is made aware, so are attorneys looking to bring together victims in a class action suit. You will need detailed records of how the breach occurred to defend your organization, and that is what forensics is all about.

Equally important in your response to the breach is how you manage the public relations nightmare that may follow and its impact on your organization's reputation. Without an independent forensic analysis, the public may jump to the conclusion that you are trying to cover up the facts. Krone explains the matter this way: "A forensic response should be part of your positive spin, that this is what's expected, this is of serious importance, and this is an important thing to do... Forensics is becoming something organizations have to do, in addition to hiring a PR firm, setting up help lines, etc."

Incident responders and/or forensics specialists may isolate an infected laptop, for instance, from your main computer network, make a copy of its storage media and use a variety of software applications to look for hidden folders, and damaged or encrypted files. They may also analyze deleted files and audit logs to trace a hacker's movements and look for internet search histories that suggest that the suspected hacker was "casing" your organization to look for weaknesses.

Even a superficial look at how a cyberattack is constructed will provide convincing evidence for the need of a forensics analysis once at a data breach has been detected. Often a data breach happens because an easy-to-find online door is left open for hackers to gain access. But some hacks start with a great deal of research—performed over many months—as hackers look for weaknesses in your computer systems, become familiar with your staffers and their responsibilities, and do Internet searches to learn everything possible about your organization. Some attacks start with phishing emails, password cracking, phone calls from persons pretending to be an internal computer technician who needs your online credentials, to name a few possibilities. Once the intruder gains entry into your network, a phase that security specialist Sean Murphy refers to as "external delivery", the next step is to set up a "Command and Control" center as a base of operations within your computer system [11].

That is the stage in which the thief looks to gain deeper access and more user privileges. If he or she succeeds, they eventually take over more advanced functions within the network and may take control of more machines on the network. Eventually, they reach their final goal, which may be to steal credit card information and medical data on patients or establish a "denial of service" (DoS) interruption on your computers that blocks access to your legitimate users. The latter can be done to simply disrupt your everyday activities, or to hold all your data for ransom. (It is worth noting that many attackers use a much simpler approach to create a DoS. They send out so many authentication requests to a web site that it overwhelms the servers.)

DECISION MAKING, ACCOUNTABILITY, AND TRUST

Throughout this book, I have talked about the importance of decision makers in healthcare playing a larger role in data security and investing in stronger encryption, malware protection, and so on. But the plain truth is *everyone* in a healthcare organization is a decision maker and shares accountability for the safety of patient information.

The mail room clerk who opens up an X-rated web site on a hospital workstation is deciding to put PHI at risk. So is the administrative assistant who opens an infected email because she cannot resist a sale on the latest shoe fashions. Similarly the staff physician who carelessly leaves her practice laptop exposed on the front seat of her car is making a decision to put patients in harm's way.

Unfortunately, all these decision makers do not relieve the top decision makers in a hospital, practice, or health insurance company of their responsibility to protect patient information. And a growing number of corporate boards are now holding these senior managers accountable. When asked the question: "Who do you hold accountable when a major breach occurs at your company?" a survey of board directors conducted in May, 2015, put CEOs at the top of their list, followed by chief information officers, the entire executive team, and chief information security officers (CISO), in descending order [12]. It is worth noting that the executive most directly responsible for cybersecurity is only listed 4th in the survey.

The *Fortune* article that reported the survey also pointed out that more than 80% of board directors discuss cybersecurity at nearly every meeting: "Two-thirds say they're 'less than confident' that their organizations are properly secured against cyber intrusions—versus a measly 4% that are 'very confident.'

Chris Wysopal, chief technology officer and CISO at Veracode, takes the view that "While the CEO isn't expected to understand the technical implications of cybersecurity, he or she is responsible for empowering those that do to speak up and to provide support for initiatives that will ultimately reduce the risk... The C-suite needs to start becoming active in these conversations, and not 'tune out' when the topic comes up in the boardroom." [13].

Tuning in to the value of cybersecurity means putting more dollars into this area, it means acting as a security champion for staff physicians who maintain they do not have the time to make security a priority because patient care is their number one priority. And it means reengineering the medical culture through staff training, email campaigns, fake phishing scams, and whatever else is needed to turn this ship around. Patient care is a sacred trust, and protecting patient information is one way to prove to patients that we consider it a privilege to maintain that trust.

References

[1] Experian Data Breach Resolution 2014-2015 Edition. http://www.experian.com/assets/data-breach/brochures/2014-2015-data-breach-response-guide.pdf.

[2] HealthData Management. 10 largest healthcare cyberattacks of 2015. http://www.health-datamanagement.com/gallery/ten-largest-healthcare-cyber-attacks-of-2015-51697-1.html?utm_medium=email&ET=healthdatamanagement:e5698345:4211341a:&utm_source=newsletter&utm_campaign=daily-dec%2010%202015&st=email.

[3] Legal Information Institute. 45 CFR 164.308 - Administrative safeguards. https://www.law.cornell.edu/cfr/text/45/164.308.

[4] T.W. Herzig, T. Walsh, L. Gallagher, Implementing Information Security in Healthcare, HIMSS, Chicago, 2013, p. 253.

[5] Federal Register. Vol 78, No 17. https://www.gpo.gov/fdsys/pkg/FR-2013-01-25/pdf/2013-01073.pdf, 2013.

[6] HHS.gov. Breach notification rule: definition of breach. http://www.hhs.gov/ocr/privacy/hipaa/administrative/breachnotificationrule/.

[7] Experian. Experian data breach resolution. http://www.experian.com/business-services/data-breach-protection.html.

[8] TransUnion. Data beach services. http://www.transunion.com/solution/data-breach-services.

[9] Equifax. Data breach services. http://www.equifax.com/help/data-breach-solutions/.

[10] M. McNickle. 5 reasons to use forensics, Healthcare IT News. http://www.healthcareitnews.com/news/5-reasons-use-forensics, 2012.

[11] S.E. Murphy, Healthcare Information Security and Privacy, McGraw Hill, New York, 2015, pp. 284–286.

[12] R. Hackett. Here's who boardrooms are blaming for data breaches, Fortune. http://fortune.com/2015/05/29/boardroom-data-breach-blame/, 2015.

[13] R. Abel. Survey: boards hold CEO most accountable when breaches occur, SC Magazine. http://www.scmagazine.com/boards-members-view-ceo-as-more-responsible-for-breaches-than-ciso-and-it-team/article/418020/, 2015.

Appendix

SAMPLE BUSINESS ASSOCIATE AGREEMENT PROVISIONS [1]

Definitions

Catch-all definition:

The following terms used in this Agreement shall have the same meaning as those terms in the HIPAA Rules: Breach, Data Aggregation, Designated Record Set, Disclosure, Health Care Operations, Individual, Minimum Necessary, Notice of Privacy Practices, Protected Health Information, Required by Law, Secretary, Security Incident, Subcontractor, Unsecured Protected Health Information, and Use.

Specific definitions:

1. Business associate: "Business Associate" shall generally have the same meaning as the term "business associate" at 45 CFR 160.103, and in reference to the party to this agreement, shall mean [Insert Name of Business Associate].
2. Covered entity. "Covered Entity" shall generally have the same meaning as the term "covered entity" at 45 CFR 160.103, and in reference to the party to this agreement, shall mean [Insert Name of Covered Entity].
3. HIPAA rules. "HIPAA Rules" shall mean the Privacy, Security, Breach Notification, and Enforcement Rules at 45 CFR Part 160 and Part 164.

Obligations and Activities of Business Associate

Business associate agrees to do the following:

1. Not use or disclose protected health information other than as permitted or required by the Agreement or as required by law;
2. Use appropriate safeguards, and comply with Subpart C of 45 CFR Part 164 with respect to electronic protected health information, to prevent use or disclosure of protected health information other than as provided for by the Agreement;

3. Report to covered entity any use or disclosure of protected health information not provided for by the Agreement of which it becomes aware, including breaches of unsecured protected health information as required at 45 CFR 164.410, and any security incident of which it becomes aware;

[The parties may wish to add additional specificity regarding the breach notification obligations of the business associate, such as a stricter timeframe for the business associate to report a potential breach to the covered entity and/or whether the business associate will handle breach notifications to individuals, the HHS Office for Civil Rights (OCR), and potentially the media, on behalf of the covered entity.]

4. In accordance with 45 CFR 164.502(e)(1)(ii) and 164.308(b)(2), if applicable, ensure that any subcontractors that create, receive, maintain, or transmit protected health information on behalf of the business associate agree to the same restrictions, conditions, and requirements that apply to the business associate with respect to such information;

5. Make available protected health information in a designated record set to the [Choose either "covered entity" or "individual or the individual's designee"] as necessary to satisfy covered entity's obligations under 45 CFR 164.524;

[The parties may wish to add additional specificity regarding how the business associate will respond to a request for access that the business associate receives directly from the individual (such as whether and in what time and manner a business associate is to provide the requested access or whether the business associate will forward the individual's request to the covered entity to fulfill) and the timeframe for the business associate to provide the information to the covered entity.]

6. Make any amendment(s) to protected health information in a designated record set as directed or agreed to by the covered entity pursuant to 45 CFR 164.526, or take other measures as necessary to satisfy covered entity's obligations under 45 CFR 164.526;

[The parties may wish to add additional specificity regarding how the business associate will respond to a request for amendment that the business associate receives directly from the individual (such as whether and in what time and manner a business associate is to act on the request for amendment or whether the business associate will forward the individual's request to the covered entity) and the timeframe for the business associate to incorporate any amendments to the information in the designated record set.]

7. Maintain and make available the information required to provide an accounting of disclosures to the [Choose either "covered entity" or "individual"] as necessary to satisfy covered entity's obligations under 45 CFR 164.528;

[The parties may wish to add additional specificity regarding how the business associate will respond to a request for an accounting of disclosures that the business associate receives directly from the individual (such as whether and in what time and manner the business associate is to provide the accounting of disclosures to the individual or whether the business associate will forward the request to the covered entity) and the timeframe for the business associate to provide information to the covered entity.]

8. To the extent the business associate is to carry out one or more of covered entity's obligation(s) under Subpart E of 45 CFR Part 164, comply with the requirements of Subpart E that apply to the covered entity in the performance of such obligation(s); and

9. Make its internal practices, books, and records available to the Secretary for purposes of determining compliance with the HIPAA Rules.

Permitted Uses and Disclosures by Business Associate

1. Business associate may only use or disclose protected health information

    [Option 1 – Provide a specific list of permissible purposes.]

    [Option 2 – Reference an underlying service agreement, such as "as necessary to perform the services set forth in Service Agreement."]

    [In addition to other permissible purposes, the parties should specify whether the business associate is authorized to use protected health information to de-identify the information in accordance with 45 CFR 164.514(a)–(c). The parties also may wish to specify the manner in which the business associate will de-identify the information and the permitted uses and disclosures by the business associate of the de-identified information.]

2. Business associate may use or disclose protected health information as required by law.

3. Business associate agrees to make uses and disclosures and requests for protected health information

    [Option 1] consistent with covered entity's minimum necessary policies and procedures.

    [Option 2] subject to the following minimum necessary requirements: [Include specific minimum necessary provisions that are consistent with the covered entity's minimum necessary policies and procedures.]

4. Business associate may not use or disclose protected health information in a manner that would violate Subpart E of 45 CFR Part 164 if done by covered entity [if the Agreement permits the business associate to use or disclose protected health information for its own management and administration and legal responsibilities or for data aggregation services

as set forth in optional provisions (e), (f), or (g) given subsequently, then add ", except for the specific uses and disclosures set forth below."]

5. [Optional] Business associate may use protected health information for the proper management and administration of the business associate or to carry out the legal responsibilities of the business associate.

6. [Optional] Business associate may disclose protected health information for the proper management and administration of business associate or to carry out the legal responsibilities of the business associate, provided the disclosures are required by law, or business associate obtains reasonable assurances from the person to whom the information is disclosed that the information will remain confidential and used or further disclosed only as required by law or for the purposes for which it was disclosed to the person, and the person notifies business associate of any instances of which it is aware in which the confidentiality of the information has been breached.

7. [Optional] Business associate may provide data aggregation services relating to the health care operations of the covered entity.

Provisions for Covered Entity to Inform Business Associate of Privacy Practices and Restrictions

1. [Optional] Covered entity shall notify business associate of any limitation(s) in the notice of privacy practices of covered entity under 45 CFR 164.520, to the extent that such limitation may affect business associate's use or disclosure of protected health information.

2. [Optional] Covered entity shall notify business associate of any changes in, or revocation of, the permission by an individual to use or disclose his or her protected health information, to the extent that such changes may affect business associate's use or disclosure of protected health information.

3. [Optional] Covered entity shall notify business associate of any restriction on the use or disclosure of protected health information that covered entity has agreed to or is required to abide by under 45 CFR 164.522, to the extent that such restriction may affect business associate's use or disclosure of protected health information.

Permissible Requests by Covered Entity

[Optional] Covered entity shall not request business associate to use or disclose protected health information in any manner that would not be permissible under Subpart E of 45 CFR Part 164 if done by covered entity. [Include an exception if the business associate will use or disclose protected health information for, and the agreement includes provisions for, data aggregation or management and administration and legal responsibilities of the business associate.]

Term and Termination

1. Term. The Term of this Agreement shall be effective as of [Insert effective date], and shall terminate on [Insert termination date or event] or on the date covered entity terminates for cause as authorized in paragraph (b) of this section, whichever is sooner.

2. Termination for cause. Business associate authorizes termination of this Agreement by covered entity, if covered entity determines business associate has violated a material term of the Agreement [and business associate has not cured the breach or ended the violation within the time specified by covered entity]. [Bracketed language may be added if the covered entity wishes to provide the business associate with an opportunity to cure a violation or breach of the contract before termination for cause.]

3. Obligations of business associate upon termination.

   [Option 1 – if the business associate is to return or destroy all protected health information upon termination of the agreement]

   Upon termination of this Agreement for any reason, business associate shall return to covered entity [or, if agreed to by covered entity, destroy] all protected health information received from covered entity, or created, maintained, or received by business associate on behalf of covered entity, that the business associate still maintains in any form. Business associate shall retain no copies of the protected health information.

   [Option 2—if the agreement authorizes the business associate to use or disclose protected health information for its own management and administration or to carry out its legal responsibilities and the business associate needs to retain protected health information for such purposes after termination of the agreement]

   Upon termination of this Agreement for any reason, business associate, with respect to protected health information received from covered entity, or created, maintained, or received by business associate on behalf of covered entity, shall:

   a. Retain only that protected health information which is necessary for business associate to continue its proper management and administration or to carry out its legal responsibilities;

   b. Return to covered entity [or, if agreed to by covered entity, destroy] the remaining protected health information that the business associate still maintains in any form;

   c. Continue to use appropriate safeguards and comply with Subpart C of 45 CFR Part 164 with respect to electronic protected health information to prevent use or disclosure of the protected health information, other than as provided for in this Section, for as long as business associate retains the protected health information;

    d. Not use or disclose the protected health information retained by business associate other than for the purposes for which such protected health information was retained and subject to the same conditions set out at [Insert section number related to previous paragraphs (e) and (f) under "Permitted Uses and Disclosures By Business Associate"] which applied prior to termination; and

    e. Return to covered entity [or, if agreed to by covered entity, destroy] the protected health information retained by business associate when it is no longer needed by business associate for its proper management and administration or to carry out its legal responsibilities.

    [The agreement also could provide that the business associate will transmit the protected health information to another business associate of the covered entity at termination, and/or could add terms regarding a business associate's obligations to obtain or ensure the destruction of protected health information created, received, or maintained by subcontractors.]

4. Survival. The obligations of business associate under this Section shall survive the termination of this Agreement.

Miscellaneous [Optional]

1. [Optional] Regulatory references. A reference in this Agreement to a section in the HIPAA Rules means the section as in effect or as amended.

2. [Optional] Amendment. The Parties agree to take such action as is necessary to amend this Agreement from time to time as is necessary for compliance with the requirements of the HIPAA Rules and any other applicable law.

3. [Optional] Interpretation. Any ambiguity in this Agreement shall be interpreted to permit compliance with the HIPAA Rules.

References

[1] HHS.gov., Business associate contracts, Sample business associate agreement provisions. http://www.hhs.gov/hipaa/for-professionals/covered-entities/sample-business-associate-agreement-provisions/index.html

Subject Index

A

Access control, 63
  approaches, 63
  role-based, 63
Accreditation groups, 116
ACMHS. *See* Anchorage Community
  Mental Health Services
  (ACMHS)
Actuarial services, 116
Addressable implementation
  specifications, 45
Administrative services, 116
Administrative staff, 103
Administrators, 60
AHIMA. *See* American Health
  Information Management
  Association (AHIMA)
American Health Information
  Management Association
  (AHIMA), 37, 65
American Medical Association,
  24, 56
  FAQ section, 24
Anchorage Community Mental
  Health Services (ACMHS), 7
Android phones, 81
Anthem
  massive data breach at, 21
Antimalware/antiviral software,
  61–62
  disadvantages of programs, 62
  vendors, 62
Antimalware programs, 52, 65, 78
Antimalware software, 86
Apple computers, 15
Auditing computer systems, 64
Audit trail management tools, 65
Authentication procedure, 55
Availability, 34

B

BAs. *See* Business associates (BAs)
BCBST. *See* BlueCross BlueShield of
  Tennes (BCBST)
Behavioural change, 107
Behavioural intentions, 107
Beth Israel Deaconess Medical
  Center, 56
Big Data, 68–70
Biometric scan, 55
Black market, 51
BlueCross BlueShield of Tennessee
  (BCBST), 12
Breach notification law, 30
Browser, 62
Budgets, 51
Business associates (BAs), 21, 42, 48,
  51, 98, 116
  contracts between, 122
  healthcare organization, 118
  patient data, 118
  protected health information,
    118
  standards, 119

C

Centers for Medicare and Medicaid
  Services (CMS), 13, 35
  analysis tools, 40
  audits, statistics on, 35
Certified information systems security
  professional (CISSP), 86
Certified in Healthcare Privacy and
  Security, 37
CFR. *See* Code of Federal Regulations
  (CFR)
Checklist, 29, 47
Chief information security officers
  (CISOs), 1, 131

CISO. *See* Chief information security
  officers (CISOs)
CISSP. *See* Certified information
  systems security professional
  (CISSP)
Clinical engineering, 100
Clinicians, 13, 104
Cloud-based email system, 41
CMS auditor, 42
Coalfire, 40
Code of Federal Regulations (CFR),
  126
  45.CFR Section164, 43
  45.CFR Section 164.302-Section
    164.308, 43
  regulations on protecting
    ePHI, 43
  regulations related to healthcare
    privacy and security, 43
Colonoscopy, 104
Communication, 23, 60
  pathways, 60
Complaints, 25
Compliance *vs.* management,
  34–36
CompTIA Security+certification
  guide, 59
Computer code, 86
Computerized provider order entry
  (CPOE), 106
Computer network, 60, 94, 104
  protection, 76
Computer operating system, 51
Confidentiality, 34
Contingency planning, 56
CPHIMS credentials, 37
CPOE. *See* Computerized provider
  order entry (CPOE)
Credit card numbers, 51
C-suite executives, 40, 56

139

Cyberattacks, 89, 125
  drill, 53
  on healthcare system, 125
Cyber criminals, 94
Cybersecurity, 19, 30, 103, 132
  budget for, 51
  insurance, 72
  insurance firm, 29
  Montana, amended breach
    notification law, 30
  national legislature, role in
    improving, 30
Cyber thieves, 51

D

Data aggregation, 116
Data analytics, 116
Data breaches, 8, 52, 77, 99, 104, 125
  discovery of, 128
  external experts, 128
  forensic root cause analysis, 129
  internal response team, assembly
    of, 128
  investigation and remediation, 128
  law enforcement agencies, 128
  normal business operations, 128
  public announcement, 128
  regulatory agencies, notification,
    128
  related lawsuits, 12
  response mechanism, 128
  response plan, 128
  violations, 8
Data deidentification services, 116
Data transfer, 60
Decision making, 131
  business leaders, 1
Default passwords, 94
Defense in Depth, 87
Denial of service (DoS), 130
Department of Health and Human
  Services (HHS), 5
Diagnostic codes, 21
Digital fingerprints of malware, 62
Digital key, 87
Digital virus, 61
DoS. *See* Denial of service (DoS)
Dropbox, 38

E

Educational specialist, 109
EHRs. *See* Electronic health records
  (EHRs)

Electronic devices, 48
Electronic format, 22, 23
Electronic health records (EHRs),
  22, 104
  internet-hosted *vs.* office-based, 38
  system, 23
  technology, 104
Electronic medical record
  systems, 105
Electronic protected health
  information (ePHI), 7, 22
Electronic records, 65
Emails, 38, 52, 65
  recipients, 52
  security, 65–67
Encryption, 4, 8, 52, 57–58, 84, 131
  protocols, 56
Enforcement rule, 22
ePHI. *See* Electronic protected health
  information (ePHI)
Establishing
  effective governance, 56
  physical safeguards, 67–68
Executives, 33
Expected utility hypothesis, 107

F

Facebook.com, 59
Facility User Access List of workforce
  members, 48
Faux malicious link, 53
Faxing, 23
  solutions, 64
FDA cybersecurity guidelines, 92
  appropriate authentication, 93
  automatic timed methods, 93
  devices, limit access, 93
  password protection strengthening,
    93
  secure data transfer, 94
  software updates restriction, 94
  user authentication, 93
Federal Bureau of Investigation, 94
Federal Trade Commission (FTC),
  28, 115
  role of, 28–29
File sharing, 82
FileVault2, 15
Financial transaction services, 120
Firewalls, 52, 58–61, 65, 82, 91
  management, 59
  types of, 59
Firmware, 97

"Flag" check box, 47
Forensics, 129
Formal agreements, 118
Fraudulent bills, 51
FTC. *See* Federal Trade Commission
  (FTC)

G

Geographic details, 19
Google docs, 60
Governance, 56, 99
Government regulations, 34
*Guide for Conducting Risk
  Assessments*, 40
*Guide to Computer Security Log
  Management*, 65

H

Hackers, 34, 52, 59
Health and Human Services (HHS),
  19, 110, 114, 127
  define identifiable health
    information, 19
  designated record sets, 23
  emphasis on documenting results
    of your risk analysis, 41
  HIPAA compliance with, 29
  patient identifiers, considered by,
    19
  PHI privacy, 21
  tapping resources, 43–45
    administrative, 44
    physical, 44
    technical, 44
  text-based user guide, 48
  training materials, 30
Healthcare clearinghouses, 19
Healthcare community, 3
Healthcare decision makers, 129
Health care ID numbers, 21
Healthcare Information Management
  Systems Society (HIMSS), 3,
  37, 96
  tool/sample analysis as an Excel
    file, 41
Healthcare IT Security, 25
Healthcare organizations, 14, 38, 42,
  49, 51, 55, 60, 127
  needs and capabilities of, 25
  rules, 22
  use and disclose PHI, 23
Healthcare professionals, 23
Health care quality, 106

Healthcare security, 89
Healthcare services, 7
Health information, 4, 22
  OCR guidelines, 22
  role of healthcare organizations, 22
Health Information Technology for Economic and Clinical Health (HITECH), 2, 4, 99, 113
  Act, 42
Health Insurance Portability and Accountability Act (HIPAA), 2, 4, 109, 113, 127
  awareness programs, 109
  breach notification rule, 27–28
  compliance issues, 108
  data breach, 19, 110
  employee training, 16
  enforcing regulations, 25
  healthcare clearinghouses, 116
  privacy and security compliance, 109
  Privacy Rule, 20, 23
  privacy training, 24
  Privacy vs. Security Rules, 22
  regulations, 6, 25, 113
  requiring audit controls, as stated in standard 164.308(a)(1)(ii)(D), 65
  rules, 6
  security rule, 26–27
  violation, 19, 94, 110, 127
  violations, 121
Health insurer, 12
Health plans, 19
Health problems, 23
Heartbleed bug, 96
HHS. See Health and Human Services (HHS)
HHS Office of Civil Rights, 43
HHS Office of General Counsel, 43
HIMSS. See Healthcare Information Management Systems Society (HIMSS)
HIPAA. See Health Insurance Portability and Accountability Act (HIPAA)
HIPAA/HITECH rules, 121
HITECH. See Health Information Technology for Economic and Clinical Health (HITECH)
Hospitals, 14, 89
  security regulations, 14

I
Idaho State University (ISU), 60
  fined for allowing unauthorized access to ePHI, 60
  Office of Civil Rights report on, 60
ID badges, 55
Infected email link, 104
Information security, 100, 126
Information technology, 15
Information technology (IT) professionals, 1
Integrity, 34
Internet, 42, 60, 77
Internet of Things (IoT), 95
Internet service provider (ISP), 59
Intrusion detection system, 63
  consists of, 64
Intrusion prevention system, 63
IoT. See Internet of Things (IoT)
IP address, 59, 60
IT professional's Guide, 1
IT research, 40

L
LANs. See Local area networks (LANs)
Local area networks (LANs), 84

M
Malicious computer code, 60
Malicious content, 60
Malware, 7, 34
Management strategy, 75
Manufacturer Disclosure Statement for Medical Device Security (MDS²), 95
McAfee, 62
MDM. See Mobile device management (MDM)
MDS². See Manufacturer Disclosure Statement for Medical Device Security (MDS²)
Media streaming, 83
Medical device
  hijacking, 90
  regulation, 91
  security, 89
    remote control, 90
    security protections, 90
    threat, 90
    vulnerabilities, 95
Medical equipment, 51

Medical errors, 104
Medical identity information, 51
Medical information, 21
Medical malpractice, 129
Medical practices, 89
Medical providers, 19, 24
Medical records, 22, 24
  information, 30
Medical staff, 103
Medicare, 51
Medjacking, 90
Microsoft Excel, 48
Mobile device management (MDM), 80
  containerize, 81
  features, 81
  platform, 81
  programs, 80
  sandbox, 81
  security safeguards, 82
    disable media streaming, 83
    file and printer sharing, turn off, 82
    network discovery, turn off, 82
    public folder sharing, turn off, 82
  services, 81
  software, 80
Mobile device management software, 52
Mobile devices, 75
  encryption, 77
  malware infection, risk of, 75
  unsecured Wi-Fi network, 75
  untrustworthy mobile app, 75

N
National Electrical Manufacturers Association, 96
National Institute of Standards and Technology (NIST), 40, 83
NEJM web site, 59
Network access server, 84
Network security, 89
NIST. See National Institute of Standards and Technology (NIST)
Norton's Internet Security, 62

O
OCR. See Office of Civil Rights (OCR)
OCTAVE approach, 41

Office of Civil Rights (OCR), 26,
        77, 114
    emphasis on documenting results
        of your risk analysis, 41
    legal right to move from civil to
        criminal action, 26
    web site, 20, 25
Office of the National Coordinator
        for Health Information
        Technology (ONC), 36, 40
    guide to privacy and security of
        electronic health information,
        36, 38
    7-step approach to security
        management, 36–40
OHCAs. *See* Organized health care
        arrangements (OHCAs)
Omnibus Rule, 42
Omnibus Security rule, 48
Online dose calculator, 60
Operating systems, 90
    outdated, 91
    Windows 7, 90
    Windows XP, 90
Organization, 22
    reputation, 2
Organized health care arrangements
        (OHCAs), 120

P

Packet filters, 59, 60
Passwords, 53
    cracking program, 54
    generation technology, 54
    policy, 53
    two-factor authentication, 55
Patient data, 12, 52, 77, 120
Patient information protection,
        110
Patient safety, 89, 106
pdf file, 48
Peer-to-peer network (P2P), 82
Personally identifiable information
        (PII), 15
PHI. *See* Protected health
        information (PHI)
Phishing, 34, 104
    email, 53
    scams, 52
Physicians, 104
    leaders, 129
PII. *See* Personally identifiable
        information (PII)
Planned behavior, 107

PMA. *See* Premarket approval
        application (PMA)
Policies, 1
Ports, 59
P2P. *See* Peer-to-peer network (P2P)
Practice management, 116
    program, 38
    software, 41
    system, 45
Premarket approval application
        (PMA), 92
Principle Logic, 40
Privacy, 126
    notification, 23
    Rule, 22, 23
    safeguards, 33
    training, 109
    violation, 23
Private practice, 15
Protected health information (PHI),
        1, 4, 19, 33, 113, 126
    define by HHS, 19
    to prevent breach, 51
Protecting big data, 68–70
Protection motivation, theory of, 107
Protocols, 59
Public-which, 2

Q

Quality Health Claims Consultants,
        24

R

Reasonably anticipated risks, 40
Reasoned action, 107
Recertification, 92
Repricing, 116
Reputation-based security, 62
Revenue cycle management
        system, 38
Risk analysis, 33
    process, 41
    tools, 40
    vendors, 40
Risk assessment, 16
Risk identification, 100
Risk management, 100
    plan, 16
Robust governance, 100

S

Safe browsing, 86
Sample analysis, 42

Secure browser connection, 77
Secure sockets layer (SSL), 42, 85
Security assessment, 14
Security Audits of Electronic Health
        Information, 65
Security awareness, 103
Security conscious culture, 51
Security governance, 56
Security incident, 7, 126
    communication, 126
    privacy, 126
Security measures, 19
Security risks, 100
    analysis, 51
    intentional, 100
    unintentional, 100
Security Rule, 22
Security specialists, 125
Security system, 14, 16
    cost of, 14
Security threats, 62
Security training resources, 110
Self-efficiency, theory of, 107
Sensitive data, 59
Servers, 65
Sexually transmitted disease, 16
    cost-effective solution, 16
    risks, 16
    transmission, 16
Signature-based malware
        program, 62
Smart card, 55
Social engineering, 52, 53
Social Security Administration, 119
Social security numbers, 21, 24
Spear phishing, 52. *See also* Phishing
Spyware, 61
SRA tool, 38, 43
    administrative regulations, 43
        CFR Sections 164.308, 164.314,
            and 164.316, 43
    download executable file containing
        the program onto, 43
    familiarize with tabs, 45
    physical regulations, 43
        Section 164.310, 43
    "required" *vs.* "addressable"
        confusion, 45–47
        HIPAA regulation 164.312(e)
            (1), 46
        risk mitigation strategy, 46
    screen capture of the graphic user
        interface, 43
        administrative question, 43

technical regulations, 43
  Section 164.312, 43
  tutorial snapshot, 44
SSL. *See* Secure sockets layer (SSL)
SSLv3 security, 96
Standards for electronic
  transactions, 22
State attorneys general, 30
State laws, 30
  amendments, 30
  Consumer Protection Act, 30
  to improve cybersecurity, 30
  inform individuals, and security
    breach, 30
  law that make a failure to notify
    consumers of a data breach, 30
5 step plan, 75
  assess, 75
  decide, 75
  develop, document, and
    implement, 75
  identify, 75
  train, 75
Symantec endpoint protection, 62

T
Technological solutions, 56
Technological tools, 1, 52. *See also*
  SRA tool
Testing network security, 70–71
Text messages, 38

Thin client, 80
Threats, 42
  vs. risk, 34
Three Ps: Passwords, policies, and
    procedures, 53
Toolkits, 40
Training
  materials, 56
  process, management, 109
  program, 51
Trend Micro report, 52
Trojan, 61

U
Unauthorized access of data, 42
Uniform resource locator (URL), 85
Unique Identifier Standards, 22
Universal plug and play, 95
Universal resource locators
    (URL), 19
University of Pittsburgh Medical
    Center (UPMC), 106
Unscrupulous security wizard, 56
UPMC. *See* University of Pittsburgh
    Medical Center (UPMC)
URL. *See* Uniform resource locator
    (URL)
US Department of Health and
    Human Services. *See* Health
    and Human Services (HHS)
User authentication, 52, 53

V
Virtual private network (VPN), 42,
    77, 83
  advantages, 83
  security protocols, 84
    IPSec, 84
    PPP, 84
    SSL, 84
  security provided by, 84
  virtues of, 83
VPN. *See* Virtual private network
    (VPN)
Vulnerabilities, 34, 42
  to email and Internet scams, 52
  in HIMSS sample risk analysis, 42

W
Wall of Shame, 24
Web server, 59
Web site, 52
  malicious, 42
Wi-Fi connection, 95
Windows phones, 81
Workstations, 65

X
X-rated web site, 131

Y
Youtube.com, 59

Printed in the United States
By Bookmasters